Having known the Selfridges from before my time at the Bible school in Scotland, and then having met several times more – last but not least at the very base where they served the Lord and where they were so much loved by the Africans in Malawi – it is such a pleasure for me to recommend this book.

We met during our Open Doors Love Africa Congress in Malawi. But it is one thing to have a conference, it is something else to really love Africans, live among them and minister the love of Jesus to them. That is what these brave souls from Scotland did and I count it an honour to be their friend.

Please read this book!
Brother Andrew

Jack Selfridge is sensitive to the needs of all he meets and as an evangelist never fails to challenge with the transforming ministry of Jesus Christ. It was my joy to get to know Jack and Isobel in Malawi where they moved quietly with a great sense of purpose.

Very Rev. Andrew B. Doig

ACKNOWLEDGEMENTS

Thanks to Isabel, my dear co-labourer during our interesting life of service together for our Lord and Master. Apart from her faithful and loving support, under very difficult travelling and living conditions, these years of missionary work would not have taken place! She wrote one or two items and also agreed to read, comment on, and correct the manuscript.

I would also like to express our appreciation for our daughter Ruth's helpful attitude as she grew up with us in such unusual circumstances! For five years she had the same person as mother at night and teacher during the day, and when she later went to boarding school, she only saw us two times each year. At school she was an 'M.K.' (Missionary Kid), the name given to children of missionaries by students who had more of this world's goods!

Thanks also to the following:

Dawn Beatty and Catherine Mackenzie who spent many hours typing the manuscript,

Dr Cundy for writing the foreword and suggesting the title.

The many missionaries of different Missionary Societies as well as the local church workers with whom we had such wonderful Christian fellowship, and who were a great help and encouragement to us in our travels in the different parts of Africa.

JACK OF ALL TRADES MASTERED BY ONE

JACK SELFRIDGE

Ps 91:1,2

Jack Selfridge

CHRISTIAN FOCUS

This book is dedicated to

ALL OUR SPIRITUAL
CHILDREN AND GRANDCHILDREN
IN AFRICA

All royalties from this book
will go to missionary work

ISBN 1 85792 281 6

Published in 1996 by Christian Focus Publications,
Geanies House, Fearn, Ross-shire, IV20 1TW
Great Britain.

Cover design by Donna Macleod

Printed and bound in Great Britain by
The Guernsey Press Co. Ltd., Vale, Guernsey, C.I.

Contents

Southern Africa

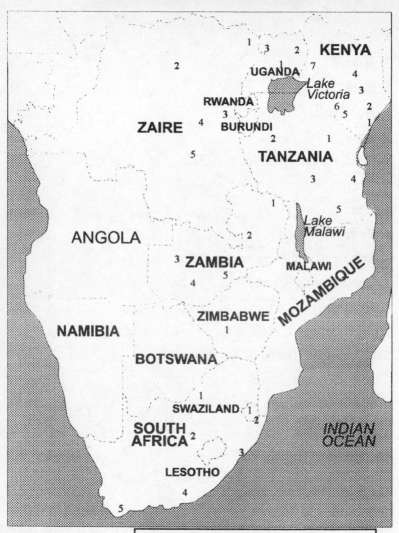

Zambia was Northern Rhodesia
Zimbabwe was Southern Rhodesia
Tanzania was Tanganyike
Zaire was the Belgian Congo
Malawi was Nyasaland

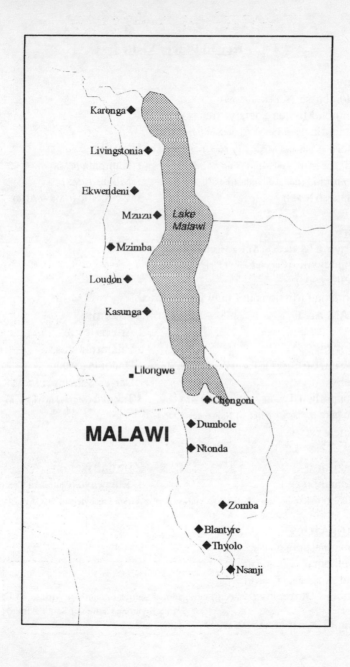

Karonga◆

Livingstonia◆

Ekwendeni◆

Mzuzu◆ *Lake*
       Malawi

◆Mzimba

Loudon◆

Kasunga◆

■Lilongwe

◆Chigngoni

◆Dumbole

◆Ntonda

MALAWI

◆Zomba

◆Blantyre

◆Thyolo

◆Nsanji

Key to Places Visited

Kenya
1 Mombassa (Salvation Army)
2 Church Mission Society Area (CMS)
3 Chigoria (Presbyterian Church of East Africa)
4 Meru (Methodist Missonary Society)
5 Kijabe (Africa Inland Mission - AIM)
6 Londiana (Londiani Industrial Mission)
7 Maneso (CMS)

Uganda
1 Kampala (CMS)
2 Mbale (CMS)
3 West Nile (CMS & AIM)

Zaire
1 Aru (AIM & Heart of Africa Mission - HAM)
2 Stanleyville (Unevangelised Fields Mission)
3 Rethy (AIM)
4 Christian Missions in Many Lands Area
5 HAM Area

Zambia
1 Mwenzo (United Church of Zambia - UCZ)
2 Lubwa (UCZ)
3 Copperbelt Towns (UCZ & CMIML)
4 Lusaka (UCZ & Church of Nazarene - CON)
5 Katete (RCZ)

Tanzania
1 Arusha (CMS)
2 Tabora (Swedish Free Mission)
3 Dodoma (CMS)
4 Dar-es-Salaam (CMS, SFM)
5 Tukuyu (Moravian Mission)

Swaziland
1 Manzini (CON)
2 Ikwezi (Metropolitan Church Association)

Zimbabwe
1 Bulawayo (Church of Central Africa Presbyterian - CCAP)

South Africa
1 Johannesburg (CON)
2 Welkom (Free Baptist Church)
3 Durban (Baptist Church)
4 Rhodes University (United Congregational Church of Southern Africa - UCCSA & Presbyterian Church of South Africa)
5 Cape Town (UCCSA & MCA)

Foreword

One day when I was working in the University of Malawi I walked into my room early to find my secretary and a friend in her office in a state of high excitement. 'You seem to be on top of the world this morning; what's happened?' 'Clement has come back to Jesus!'

The miracle, the directness, the joy expressed in those six words, all reflect the influence of the man you will meet in this book. If you think you are not likely to hear them in a similar context in reserved Britain, there is a message here for you. Read on, for the story is thrilling and challenging, and it is a privilege to write its foreword.

Here is the story of two remarkable people. Over it I want to write: 'By faith Jack ... By faith Isabel ...'. For it is a vivid modern reminder that the three Greek words usually translated 'Have faith in God' could equally well have the meaning 'Hold on to God's faithfulness'. Here is a record of 50 years of trust in God which He has singularly honoured and blessed.

The percipient reader will note the silences in this book and may find some unanswered questions. Jack, like his Master, knew the hurt of being misunderstood, yet there is no bitterness here, and this record of changed lives gives the lie to what we knew to be absurd misconceptions.

Many times I have asked a Christian student how he or she came to know the Lord. More often than not the answer would be: 'You see, a man called Jack Selfridge came to our village ...' When I came to know Jack and to share with him in some of the New Life for All ministry I understood the prevalence of such a reply. And more recently, when my wife and I went to Scourie and found on the church gate a notice 'This church is prayer conditioned', we recognized the secret behind the power of this beloved couple wherever they went.

You need a tooth extracted – a clock adjusted – a car repaired – a marriage rescued – a church planted ...? Jack's your man! Jack of all trades, mastered by One – Jesus who died for our sins, and not for our sins only, but for the sins of the whole world. Eternity alone will show how much Malawi owes to the lad from Cullybackey.

Martyn Cundy
formerly Professor of Mathematics
University of Malawi

Preface

After a period of thirty-eight years of very interesting missionary work in nine of the countries in Africa, many people have been urging us to write an account of our experiences.

Now that we are supposed to be retired, we have decided, with the Lord's help, to attempt to share some of the wonderful things Isabel and I have seen Him do during the years. However, we only do so with the desire and prayer that God will have the praise and glory, as we are His unprofitable servants.

We saw times of persecution and revival in the churches, and we witnessed the amazing grace of God in the wonderful spiritual transformation of many lives. We experienced the Lord's guidance and provision, as well as His protection, especially when threatened with death during periods of dangerous political rioting. As well as being able to share the good news of the gospel, we had many opportunities to do medical and dental work.

We pray that the account will strengthen the faith of God's people, and that non-Christians will realise that God is alive and able, through the Lord Jesus, to forgive, change and bring true joy and satisfaction to all who will surrender the complete control of their lives to Him.

Also, we long and pray that it will attract and inspire Christian men and women to answer the Saviour's call to 'Go into all the world and preach the gospel'. Millions in the world have never yet heard about Jesus!

Jack Selfridge
September 1996

MILESTONES

1921	Jack born, 10th August
1942	Jack graduates from Bible College in Glasgow
1948-1951	Jack involved in church planting in South Africa
1952	Jack and Isobel marry in November
1953-1954	First trip to Central and Southern Africa.
1955-1957	Second trip to Southern Africa. Sees revival in Malawi
1958-1970	Base Malawi
1961	Daughter Ruth born
1969	Evangelical Association of Malawi (now The Evangelical Fellowship of Malawi) ask Jack to become secretary of 'New Life For All'.
1970-1975	Move To Blantyre
1974	Dr. Hastings K Banda, President of Malawi, moves capital from Zomba to Lilongwe
1975	African colleagues take over 'New Life For All'.
1975-1979	Jack receives call to be co-minister in new Lingladzi congregation in Lilongwe
1980-1984	Jack accepts call to multiracial church in Cape Town, South Africa. During this time Ruth completes her nurse's training.
1984	Return to Malawi. Lay-training centre.
1985-1986	Return to another Lilongwe congregation as co-minister.
1986-1991	Minister of Church of Scotland congregation in Scourie in the Highlands of Scotland.
1991-	Retired. Jack engages in locum ministry, pulpit supply, and visits Africa for short teaching appointments.

1

An Exciting Life

Who said that a missionary's life must be very dull, monotonous and boring? Many young people, as well as those who are older, have formed that impression.

Having been a missionary for almost forty years, in nine countries in Africa, I can only describe missionary life as very thrilling and exciting. But you can form your own opinion after travelling with me through the following chapters. But before we go any further let me share a couple of incidents that will help to point out how 'thrilling and exciting' it can be.

Meeting A Python in the Moonlight.

One evening in Zambia, after we had completed a day of lessons for students, a young man who had been greatly helped by a book we had written entitled *Following Jesus* came to discuss some of the points in which he was interested. I accompanied him back to his hostel, but as the moon was shining brightly I did not bother to take a torch.

On the way back I was walking along a lane under some trees where the moonlight was causing shadows of the leaves to camouflage the surface. Suddenly as I glanced down, I discovered that I was about to step on a very large python. Its head had gone into grass at one side of the lane while the rest of its body had not emerged from the grass on the other side! Although a python bites, its bite does not have venom, but it has two claw-like projections near the end of its tail which can be very dangerous. With these it grips a person, and quickly coils itself round to crush its victim to death, before swallowing the crushed body.

I stepped back quickly, and as the missionary with whom I was staying had two small children, I knew that it would be very dangerous to leave the snake in the vicinity of his house. So while watching the snake from a distance, I called for someone to bring me an axe. When the axe arrived, I tried to hit the snake's head as it began to climb a tree, but had to lookout in case I received a swipe of its tail! Unfortunately the head came off the axe, not the snake, so it became very angry, but eventually with the handle of the axe, the snake was killed.

The missionary, who was away from the house at the time, was so disappointed that he had missed the opportunity to film the snake while it was still alive. My sense of humour prompted me to make the following suggestion to him. 'Charlie,' I said, 'if you want a photo of the snake I will arrange one for you!'

The next morning we went over to a large forked tree and, while I pushed the snake through the fork of the tree from a position at the back where I could not be seen, Charlie took a shot with his movie camera. I then suggested that as the film had just shown the snake moving, I should film Charlie walking up to the tree and showing great surprise on seeing the python. However, when he reached the tree and saw the snake, he pulled it out of the tree and began to wrap it round his body! I heard later that when he showed the film in his native Canada, he had some near-fainting scenes from people in his audiences.

Sentenced to Death in the Pulpit

The years from 1959 to 1962 in Malawi were years of political unrest, resulting in riots, deaths, and much civil disobedience. The local population wanted independence from the Federation of Rhodesia and Nyasaland, into which they felt they had been forced against the wishes of their leaders by the Colonial Government.

An African Presbyterian minister asked me if I would preach for him in one of his churches on a certain Sunday. I agreed as I had often taken services for him. But he did not tell me that he had been warned that if he preached in that church again he would be killed! I heard later that a group of young men in the area had announced that no more church services would be held there. They said that the church was no longer the house of God, but that it was the house of the Malawi Congress party.

Communistic influences had taken advantage of the situation, and claimed that the country had been incorporated into the Federation so that white people could take the land. They claimed that missionaries were agents of the Colonial Government and used their religion to prepare for the takeover of the land. They had been taught that religion is the opium of the people. The local Congress Party was the god they were to 'worship'.

It was interesting that during the week preceding the service, one by one, four young Christians – men who had been converted under our ministry – came and asked me if they could accompany me to the church. I agreed, and when we arrived in the village we were invited to have tea in a Christian teacher's house. He informed us that word had been spread around the parish by the young Congress men that anyone who attended church that day would be beaten.

When we entered the church, which was constructed of mud and wattle with a thatched roof, we found twenty-one people who had come to worship, in spite of the threat of being beaten. Usually there were about 150 who worshipped weekly in that little church. We sat on a raised mud platform on home-made chairs and one of the young men announced the opening hymn.

During the singing of the hymn, we heard a political song being sung in the distance outside the church. Also political slogans were being shouted. The noise grew louder, and then suddenly into the back of the church burst about thirty-five young men. As we continued to sing, they tried to drown out our voices with their songs. The leader of our hymn said to me, 'What do you think we should do?' 'We must carry on,' I said, 'because if we stop the service, they will feel that they have overcome us, and they will try to do the same in other areas where we are preaching. If we ask them to leave, there are more of them than there are of us, and they will resist violently.'

So we carried on, although the noise they were making made it very difficult to read the Scripture and pray. When I stood up to preach, they realised that they were not going to stop the service as they had boasted, and they became very angry. They marched up to the front of the church, turned to the twenty-one people in the congregation, and ordered them out of the church, threatening to beat anyone who refused to go. Not one person went out, and that gave us good support to continue the service. All the time they were threatening the congregation, I tried to 'preach over their heads' as they stood with their backs to me.

When the one who seemed to be the leader saw the courage and determination of the congregation, and the continuation of the service, he became very furious. Turning to me he said, 'If you don't stop preaching now we are going to kill you.' I ignored the threat and continued to preach, although it was difficult for the congregation to hear above the noise of the intruders. I was determined not to allow them to bring the service to an end.

That made them more angry. They snatched my Bible from me and threw it across the church where it hit the wall and broke in two. They took the Testaments and hymn books from my friends on the platform and tore them to shreds, and carried away the pulpit table. All the time I continued to preach, and was very glad that I did not have a written sermon!

Then the mob became very violent, breaking some of the chairs and using the legs to threaten us. Eventually they began to beat the local elders and, waving the legs over our heads, told us that it was our last opportunity to stop the service – otherwise we would be killed. When things reached that stage, the congregation realised that we were in danger and came up to the front to try and protect us. As there was no-one left in the seats to whom I could preach, I stopped and addressed the intruders: 'If you think that your threats will stop us from doing God's work, you are mistaken. Many people have died for Jesus, and we are willing to die for Him if it is necessary.'

I then suggested to my friends on the platform that we should drop down on our knees and pray for our attackers. I have been in many prayer meetings, but that was the best one in which I have ever taken part! With our eyes closed, we did not know at what moment we would be struck a severe or fatal blow. But the Lord filled us with such joy that we were bursting with praise to Him and raising our 'hallelujahs'. That day we learned a wonderful lesson which we will never forget. We discovered that when the time comes to die – even if it were the violent death of a martyr – the Lord supplies all the grace that is necessary to die rejoicing. We proved so wonderfully the words of Nehemiah, 'The joy of the LORD is your strength' (Nehemiah 8:10).

When all five of us had prayed, we opened our eyes and found that our attackers had withdrawn to the church door. They did not know what to do with us, for they had realized that their plans had failed to frighten us and stop the service. Instead they saw that their threats and blows had given us an occasion for great joy and rejoicing in the Lord. This they could not understand.

We sat with the members of the congregation for a short time, sharing our joy and thanking the Lord for His wonderful, watchful care over us. As we left the church, I stopped to speak to the men who had attacked us, telling them: 'We want you to know that we have forgiven you for what you have done today. You have not just attacked us, but you have attacked God by tearing His Word and trying to stop us from worshipping Him. As Jesus prayed for those who killed Him, "Father, forgive them for they know not what they do", we pray the same prayer for you today.'

On the way home from the church I could hardly keep the young men in the car, they were so full of joy. They said, 'To think that we were almost killed today but we had no fear. We had so much joy, we could have died singing.' The disciples must have had a similar experience in Acts 5:40, 41. After the Sanhedrin had arranged for them to be beaten, 'they departed ... rejoicing that they were counted worthy to suffer shame for his name ....' We discussed how God does not give grace and joy for us to sit at home and think about how we would act if threatened with death, but if the time comes, He gives us all the courage and joy that is necessary. He never shows His power and grace when it is not an appropriate time. He controls His power according to the difficulty, but not until it is required! Stephen died with his face 'like the face of an angel', praying that God would forgive those who were stoning him (Acts 6:15; 7:60).

It was wonderful to see, in later years, that all four of these young men entered the ministry of the church.

Franklin Chunga has had a number of parishes; was travelling secretary for the Student Christian Organization of Malawi; chairman of the Censorship Board of Malawi for a period; and at the time of writing has been called over to England by the Methodist church to help with evangelism.

Richard Ndolo was one of Malawi's best preachers. He worked in many large congregations. In one charge he had over sixty prayer houses. But after a long illness he died of cancer at the end of 1994.

Wyson Jere's main interest is outreach evangelism, although he too served in many parishes and had the joy of seeing many people coming to faith in Christ. He is now full-time evangelism secretary in the north of Malawi, under the Evangelical Fellowship of Malawi.

Frank Ndhlazi has faithfully served the Lord in many isolated and lonely charges and, being the youngest of the four, expects to serve a few more years yet before retiring.

But to get back to our experience in the church: Isabel was not with us in the church that day. She was pregnant and had some difficulties with the pregnancy, so the doctor had ordered her to stay in bed. We were glad that she was not with us as the experience could have caused her to lose the baby. When I got home and told her what had happened she wanted to see my Bible. 'Did you notice where it is broken?' she asked. When I informed her that I had not looked, she told me that it had been broken in Romans 12, and then she read: 'Bless them which persecute you: bless and curse not .... Recompense to no man evil for evil .... Avenge not yourselves, but rather give place unto wrath .... Vengeance is mine: I will repay, says the Lord .... If thine enemy hunger, feed him: if he thirst, give him drink .... Be not overcome of evil, but overcome evil with good.'

Some days later the chief of police in the area called me to his office. He was a white man, but also a 'white heathen'. He had no use for the church, for the Bible or for God. 'You had a riot in the village of Mpongo,' he said. 'Why did you not come and report the attack? Were you intimidated by the men who attacked you? I am going out to make arrests and I need you as a witness.'

I told him that there were two reasons why I did not report the incident and why I could not go out with him to witness against the men. First, I explained that before we left the church I had informed the men that we had forgiven them; and secondly, my Bible had been torn at a section where told me that I was to bless my attackers and not to avenge myself, but to overcome evil with good, and that vengeance belongs to the Lord and He will repay.

He was upset and said he would not be able to take any action without my help. He also told me that the magistrate was very concerned because the riot had happened in his area. The policeman said that I should go and see him. I then went and gave the magistrate my two reasons for not reporting the matter. He said, 'It may be all right for you to forgive them, Jack, but I don't need to forgive. I am going out to make arrests.'

However, he must have changed his mind, or could not find any other witness, for no legal action was ever taken against the attackers. When it was known that we had really forgiven them and refused to co-operate in having them arrested, we were invited back to the village, with apologies! In the meantime our daughter, Ruth, had been born, and all three of us went back to have a service in the village. When we arrived, we found about 500 people gathered at the church which was too small for such a number and we had to have the service in the open-air.

At the end of the service quite a number came forward to receive counsel on how to give themselves to the Lord Jesus. We could only say with Paul: 'The things that happened to us were for the furtherance of the gospel' (Philippians 1:12).

So those who think that a missionary's life is dull and unexciting are under a misconception, as many other details in the book will confirm. But you may now be wondering how I came to be a missionary in Africa.

2

How It All Began

I was born on the 10th of August, 1921 into a Christian home, for which I thank the Lord. Family worship, conducted by parents who loved the Lord, was my introduction to God's love and wonderful plan of salvation.

We lived near a little village called Cullybackey in County Antrim, Northern Ireland. That was the year in which the border was arranged between the North and South of Ireland, but as a child I do not remember any serious conflict between the Nationalist and Loyalist groups. Those were quite peaceful years compared to the twenty-five which followed 1968, during which hundreds of lives were lost through terrorism.

In fact, until I went over to Scotland to train at sixteen years of age, I only remember hearing of one murder in Ulster. I still remember the name of the man who was sentenced to death for the murder, as well as the day on which he was hanged. A feeling of gloom hung over the district and our home that day as execution was such an uncommon event. My mother was very close to tears as she talked about the prisoner and his family.

My father was a lay preacher. He organized a circuit of interdenominational cottage meetings in the area where we lived. Around twenty-six homes were involved, and the services were held fortnightly which meant that it was an annual event in each home. The householder was responsible to choose the preacher, and usually it was the family's own minister or pastor, but quite often my father was asked to preach.

My mother's parents were farmers and she was a member of a family of ten children. It was her ambition to be a teacher, but being one of the oldest children, when she finished primary school, she became involved in work in the home and on the farm. However, she was able to attend elocution classes, and when we were small she often entertained us in the evenings with fascinating poems. One of these still stands out in my memory as it described the illness and death of a little boy called Jim.

Mother had a few close brushes with death in her early years. Once she was knocked over and pressed into the soft ground by a horse drawn roller, when she went out to call her father for a meal. On rushing into the house, she received a scolding from her mother for dirtying her dress, before her father could arrive to explain what had happened. Another time she fell into a pit when out walking in a peat bog and was only rescued after a search was made. On yet another occasion she was tossed into the air by a troublesome cow. Fortunately, none of these experiences caused much harm to her physically, and looking back it is clear that the Lord had a purpose in sparing her life.

We had a very happy home life. Of course, there were no TVs, and radios were too expensive for my father's wages. 'Talkies' were taking the place of silent films in the cinemas, but there was no cinema near our country cottage. Had there been one, we would not have been allowed to attend as my parents felt that the influence of many films was detrimental to morals.

Church, Sunday School, and primary school made up most of our social life outside the home, apart from the school holidays which we spent on the two farms of our four grandparents. Usually we had one day at the seaside on our Sunday School 'excursion'. It was always a great event on holidays to travel in the bus to our grandparents, and to sit as near the driver as possible. In those early days my greatest ambition was to be a bus driver!

My father had a full-time, seven-day-week job as a cattle-man on a large estate, with a wage of twenty-seven shillings and six pence – £1.38. In his spare time he was the local cycle repairer, gents' hairdresser, and 'quack' vet! He did not charge for his services unless there was expense involved in providing cycle parts or animal medicine. Because of his generosity, though, we children had quite a few pennies slipped to us by satisfied recipients of his services.

In spite of his low income, and the fact that there were five children in the family when I was young, my parents had over fifty years of happy married life. I never remember my parents having a serious argument. They had their own way of solving their differences of opinion.

I must admit that we were brought up very strictly. We were not allowed to go to any events about which my parents had any question as to their suitability. There were no games allowed on the Sabbath, and it was not the done thing to polish shoes, trim nails, or even whistle on the Lord's Day. Today, many people think that such discipline is oppressive and boring for children, but I never remember thinking that it was so. We were glad to give one day to Jesus as we had all the other days for our own activities. We attended two Sabbath Schools and a church service each Sunday, although it meant walking a mile each way to the village.

An incident comes to mind which illustrates the discipline of the home. It took place one night when my brother and I were about eight and ten respectively. We decided that we would like to imitate a grown-up and have a 'smoke' (my parents did not smoke).

After dark, when no one was looking, my brother Andy and I got a piece of old cane and a box of matches. We went into our outside lavatory, broke the cane into two pieces, and 'lit up'! We forgot that there was a little window in the room, so each time we had a 'pull' there was quite a bright glow. As we took so long to return to the house, Father decided to go out and investigate, and the glow in the window told the story of what was happening! After finding out what we were doing, we received such a severe caning that Mother had to suggest to Father that we had had enough. That was the last 'smoke' I ever had, but not the last caning I had for other misdeeds.

Father believed wholeheartedly in Proverbs 13:24: 'He who spares the rod, hates his son: but he who loves him is careful to discipline him' (NIV). Such discipline is frowned upon in homes and schools these days, but are we not reaping the results of its disappearance? Our media almost daily has its reports of murder, rape, mugging and other crimes. We are seeing the havoc caused by an undisciplined generation.

One evening, when I was thirteen years of age, I remained behind for counselling after a service conducted in a Faith Mission evangelistic campaign. I had been convicted of various misdeeds like taking apples from someone's orchard and telling lies to my mother and my teacher. I realised that I needed to be forgiven by God and changed so that I could live a true Christian life. After I had told Jesus that I was really sorry and had asked Him to forgive and come into my life, I had the joy of knowing that He had answered, just as He had promised in Revelation 3:20: 'Behold I stand at the door and knock: if any man hears My voice, and opens the door, I will come in to him and sup with him and he with Me.'

Illness

A few months after my conversion I became seriously ill with what doctors decided was tuberculosis of the spine and I was confined to bed for five months. Most of the time I had to lie on a bed that had no pillow, with a wooden bottom, on which I had to lie on my back to avoid curvature of the spine. The prognosis was not good, as the modern drugs for tuberculosis had not been discovered in the early 1930s. From the doctors' words and attitude, I felt they had no hope for my recovery.

During my months in hospital, people who included Sabbath School teachers, scoutmaster, school friends, and others brought me books to read. I was very interested to find that many of the books were about missionary work in Africa. David Livingstone, Robert Moffat, Mary Slessor and C. T. Studd were some of God's servants whose lives were described. Reading about the incidents in their lives took me back to the time when I was eight years old. My school teacher asked the class to write an essay on the subject, 'What I would like to be when I grow up'. As I sat in school and thought about it, I decided that I would like to be a minister in the church! After that, whenever I misbehaved, the teacher took advantage of that essay to tell me that I did not always act like a minister!

Having plenty of time in hospital to contemplate, I thought much about the life of a missionary, and began to feel a deep longing to go and work for Jesus one day. That thought came to a climax when a lady gave me a magazine in which there was an account of the Lord Jesus sending for the donkey so that He could ride into Jerusalem. The magazine used the words of Jesus, when he told His disciples that if anyone tried to stop them untying the donkey they should say, 'The Lord has need of him'. The magazine then adapted the words to read, 'The Lord has need of YOU!' I suddenly felt that the Lord was saying that about me.

I took these words as a confirmation that I should offer myself to the Lord to serve Him as a missionary in Africa. But I was faced with the fact of my illness, and a suggestion, which no doubt came from Satan, that my illness was terminal. Then I prayed, 'Lord, if You ever make me well, I am willing to go to Africa and work for You there. But just as Your donkey was tied and had to be released because You needed him, I am "tied" to this bed and you will have to untie me if You need me.' I knew that it was only God who could perform the miracle and 'loose' me from the disease that held me there, if He wanted me to work for Him in Africa.

From the time I prayed that prayer, as far as I can remember, I had no more pain in my back! After another month had passed, during which I kept informing the doctors that I no longer had pain, they reluctantly gave me permission to get out of bed. They told me though, 'If you feel pain again, report back to us immediately'. But that was never necessary, for which I have thanked the Lord many times.

When I was in hospital, my father had become ill and had lost his employment on the estate. His weekly 'sick allowance' was very small – just ten shillings. Being the eldest in the family, I knew that my father would quite understandably expect me to work and bring some cash into the home. How could I get the courage to inform him that I felt God was calling me to be a missionary and to ask his permission to leave home and train for that work?

But again I had to thank the Lord for Christian parents who had dedicated and committed each of us in the family to the Lord, and prayed for us that we would love and serve Him. When I explained to my father the reasons why I felt that the Lord was calling me to missionary work, he said, 'If God is calling you to missionary work, I will not stand in your way. Go ahead and obey Him. I would not object if all my children became missionaries!' His only regret was that he could not help me with the fees for my training. We both knew, however, that if God was calling me, then it would be no problem for Him to provide what was necessary. Without any requests on my part, the fees were provided by Christian friends who heard of my call and my decision to train.

My father's desire that the other members of the family would also serve the Lord, did come to pass. All seven of us (two more children were born after I went into training) are serving the Lord in different ways. Four of us have served in overseas mission work, and the other three in Christian activities, two part and one full time.

Training

I was accepted for missionary training in the Metropolitan Bible Training School in Glasgow. The school was founded by a Canadian, Rev. Charles Fordham, who had gone to the Gold Coast (now Ghana) in West Africa to work as a missionary. At that time, around 1920, the area was known as the 'white man's grave' because of the prevalence of malaria. His wife took very ill and died there, and he had such recurrent attacks of the fever that he almost died too and had to leave.

The loss of his wife was a great blow to him, and the fact that he could no longer work there was a great disappointment. But because of his love for Africa, and the great need for missionaries at that time, as well as what he felt was a call from God, led him with some others interested in missionary work to found a school in which young men and women could be trained. Their church background was Methodist, but the school was open to people of different denominations. I came from the Presbyterian Church of Northern Ireland.

The school aimed to prepare students in three ways – spiritually, academically and practically. There were studies in the Scriptures, theology, church history, homiletics, English, Christian journalism, etc., for the preparation of our minds. There were devotional lectures, sermons, and private counselling for the upbuilding of Christian character and devotion to the Lord. And practical training included subjects like youth work and other outreach evangelism, calling in homes with Christian literature, gardening, cooking, printing, mechanics, electricity and general handymanship for the purpose of enabling the mission worker to be practical with his or her hands. Of course ladies had other subjects such as sewing and more advanced cooking.

Discipline, under the supervision of dormitory superintendents, was very strict. We were not allowed out of the grounds without permission. The rising bell rang at 6.00 am and there was one hour for personal devotions before breakfast. Lights had to be out at 10.00 pm. On no account was any friendship, or even a conversation, allowed between the opposite sexes during our training. Conversation was only allowed if the matter affected the business of the school, or was necessary for some other reason.

Although the above methods of discipline may seem very severe, I look back on them with thanks and appreciation. They built character, and helped us to avoid many things which could have distracted us from our main purpose in being in the school.

I learned one very valuable lesson while in Bible School. As I mentioned, when I was in hospital and was impressed with the story of Jesus sending for the donkey, I offered myself to Him for His service – to be His 'donkey'! But I learned that I was more stubborn than the donkey used by Jesus. No-one had ever sat on the donkey that Jesus used and yet it was willing to take Him to Jerusalem without any objection, although people were shouting and throwing clothes and branches in front of it. All donkeys are not like that; the frightening obstructions and noise would have been enough to cause a well-trained donkey to bolt and throw its rider!

I know from experience. I have been tossed over the head of one, and once when I was riding without a saddle, the donkey got a fright and went off at such speed that I fell and broke my clavicle.

I found that as a 'donkey' Jesus wanted to use, I had a will of my own. The crisis came to a head over a plan I was contemplating. I decided that a young lady who was also training would make a good wife for me in missionary work. Under the rules of the school I was not allowed to have any communication with her. As far as I know she knew nothing about my aspirations. (That was before I had seen the lovely young woman with whom I eventually fell in love and married.)

The more I exercised my mind on this plan, the colder I became spiritually – the joy of the Lord was being withdrawn.

When I realised what was happening and prayed over the matter, I saw that just as a stubborn donkey makes its own plans so I was making mine, and I expected the Lord to agree!

I then had to make a choice. Was I willing to be entirely at the Lord's disposal for the work He wanted me to do, or was I going to dictate to Him the way I wanted to serve Him? After a three month struggle I saw that just as I came to Jesus and accepted Him as my Saviour, I also had to accept Him as my Lord and Master. I had to be willing to 'die', as Paul explains, to all my own selfish plans, and carry my Master where He wanted and how He wanted. The climax came when I prayed, 'Lord, if it is Your will for me to remain single for the rest of my life so that I can win more souls for You by doing so, I will gladly accept Your will and whatever else it involves.'

It then became clear to me what Paul was urging in Romans 12:1, 2, when he wrote to the Christians in the church at Rome. Their bodies were to be completely yielded to the Holy Spirit so that He could use them to speak His words, do His work, think His thoughts, and go with His message wherever He wanted. Paul then pointed out that Christians must not conform to worldly desires, but allow their minds to be transformed. In other words, to receive the mind of Christ, as it is only then that we are able to discover the 'good and acceptable and perfect will of God' for our lives and service. In surgical language we could say that it is a 'mind transplant'.

Surrender to God's will did not just include the question of marriage for me but all other decisions that had to be made throughout my missionary life. I knew that I was a child of God, but I did not recognise the reserves and restrictions I was placing on the Holy Spirit's control of my life. The picture came to my mind that my life was like a motor car. I wished to be the driver, but wanted the Lord to sit in the back seat so that I could call on Him to take over when I was in difficulties! I had then reached a new crisis in my life – the crisis of full surrender to the Lord, which was not just a once-for-all yielding of my will, but the beginning of the need for daily yielding to the Lord's will in all of life's decisions and plans. He was to be in full control. Very often a donkey is referred to as a 'stupid ass'. As I was called into the Lord's service through the story of Jesus sending for the donkey, I realised that I was too stupid to control my own life in His service. Jesus could have chosen an intelligent horse instead of a donkey, and He could have chosen a much more intelligent person than I am. But it is encouraging to note that as far as we can surmise, Jesus travelled on a donkey three other times – to His birth place, to Egypt, and on His return to Nazareth. Not as the little boy told his Sunday school teacher that Jesus travelled to Egypt in an aeroplane, and Pontius was the Pilate!

Paul reminds us: 'Brothers, think what you were when you were called. Not many of you were wise by human standards ... God chose the foolish things of the world to shame the wise ....' (1 Corinthians 1:26, 27, NIV). One should never be ashamed to act as God's donkey.

I graduated in 1942, but the war was still being fought and it was difficult to obtain a passage overseas. Coming from Northern Ireland, where there was no conscription, I was not called up into the services, so I got involved in youth work in Ireland and Glasgow until the door opened up for me to go to Africa.

In 1947 the school where I trained was asked to suggest a missionary who could accept an appointment in South Africa for two years, under the Society in the United States which had sent Charles Fordham to Ghana. I was approached to consider the appointment, on condition that I would go to the United States for six months further training. I felt that it was the Lord's will for me to accept.

In the United States

Arriving in the United States after living in Britain during the war years with the rationing and austerity, was like entering a new world. To see piles of leftover food being tossed overboard from the ship as we crossed the Atlantic, and later from the kitchen of the Bible School, shocked me very much. I thought of how different it must be in the African villages. Also being used to petrol rationing and the economic use of cars, it was quite a sight to see dual carriageways with about eight lanes of cars going each way! It required concentration to remember to look the opposite way when crossing the road, as the traffic was travelling in the wrong direction according to my mental computer.

However, I enjoyed the study of new subjects as well as meeting with other students and the staff. Also I had the opportunity to take part in services in quite a number of different cities in the States and Canada, and made many new friends who became prayer-partners.

Travelling from Canada to New York in an overnight train when there were only two of us in the coach, the other passenger became quite drunk. In the middle of the night he staggered over to me, and asked from where I had come. I told him that I came from Ireland.

'Catholic or Protestant?' he shouted. When I told him that I was a Protestant, he closed his fist and tried to aim it at my face, which in his drunken state, he found difficult! I just had to burst out laughing as I saw the funny side of the incident that thousands of miles from Ireland the Irish question popped up in a train.

He then dropped his fist and sitting down beside me, invited me to go to Boston with him. 'There are more Irishmen in Boston than there are in Ireland,' he said. As he continued to talk, he began to swear and use the name of the Lord Jesus. 'I don't like to hear you talking about Jesus like that,' I said. 'He is my best Friend.' He then burst into tears and told me that when he was young it was his desire to train as a priest, but he had fallen into the wrong company and was living the wrong kind of life. We had a good talk on spiritual things as he seemed to sober up a little. Eventually he put his hand into his pocket and took out a large handful of dollar notes which he tried to give me. I did not take them as I knew he would be looking for them later, but I wondered many times what happened to them when he arrived in New York!

I sailed back to Scotland in the spring of 1948, and left for Africa that autumn. I was twenty-seven years of age.

3

Church Planting in South Africa

It was difficult to get an overseas passage during the war and for some years afterwards as so many people wanted to travel. The Union Castle Line served Africa at that time. They decided to use some of their ships, which had been fitted out as troopships, to transport emigrating passengers. That meant that a larger number could be accommodated. I travelled on the *Caernarvon Castle* in September 1948 to Cape Town.

There were about 1,500 of us on board. Being single, I slept in what had been a hold of the ship which was fitted out with sixty hammocks. Actually the hammocks were a good idea as they still hung plumb when the ship rolled! We queued for our three meals which were served on trays divided into sections for the different courses. However, we could not complain about the service as the fare was only £42.00 for the fifteen day trip from Southampton to Cape Town! That would not even provide a bed for one night in many of our British hotels now.

What a wonderful sight it was on the morning of the fifteenth day, to be up early and to see the majestic Table Mountain basking in the morning sun, with the city of Cape Town stretched out between the mountain and the sea. I had arrived at the entrance to the continent that was to be my home for the next thirty-eight years!

I was met on the quay side by a group of missionaries I had never seen before, and with whom I had been appointed to work. They gave me a very warm welcome, and for some time I was accommodated with them at the Mission headquarters in Cape Town. Later I moved to a smallholding, owned by the Mission,

on the outskirts of the city. While I was there, an amusing incident took place.

I had to leave early one day and left a young boy to look
after the house. He went out later and locked the door, but as he
knew that I would be back before he was, he 'hid' the key of
the door under a large oil drum on the veranda. In case I could
not find it, he drew a line in chalk from the door to the drum,
and in large letters wrote, 'Key hidden here'. His impression of
something hidden was different from mine!

I found that a large Sunday School of about 400 children
and adults had been organised by the missionaries in the village hall of the area where I had been appointed to work. I was
asked to take responsibility for the boys and young men who
attended the Sunday School. 1948 was the year in which the
Nationalist party had come to power in South Africa. Apartheid laws were being incorporated into the statute-book. These
curtailed the activities and place of abode of all persons who
were not classed as 'white'. Because of these laws, 'white' people were looked upon with suspicion by those who did not fit
into that group.

The people among whom I was to work were classed as
'coloured' in the apartheid system. They were people of mixed
race so were neither 'white' nor 'black', but because they were
not 'white' they came under the restrictions of all who were
'non-white'. For instance, the local trains had separate coaches,
some marked 'Whites only', others marked 'non-Whites'.

One day I decided to ride in a coach marked 'non-Whites'
to show to the local travellers that I was not in agreement with
the system. But when I entered, I got a shock. I was accused of
going into that coach because I could not get a seat in a 'white'
one, and I should not take advantage of their coach when they
were not allowed into ours. They could not accept the fact that
I would enter their coach because of objecting to apartheid.

The village hall in which our Sunday School was held was

in an area which had been set aside for 'coloured' people. At first it was not easy to win the confidence of the teenagers and young men and their parents. Naturally they had a chip on their shoulders as they felt they were being treated and counted as second class citizens, and they saw that I had the same shade of skin as those who were planning their segregation. However, after playing football with the boys, or climbing Table Mountain on Saturdays, relationships improved over the course of the first year.

We then went to the seaside and camped together in a large tent. At the end of the camp we had a parents' day and provided a meal for them. From that time I felt that I was looked upon as a friend and I was warmly welcomed in all the homes. In fact, being single at that time, I often came away from their homes with items of delicious home-baking! One elderly lady, who had been a cook, came around sometimes on Saturdays and cooked my Sunday lunch.

But there was a very sad side to working with these young people. Because of the segregation of the races and the fact that most secondary education, trades and professions were reserved for white people, the boys had little prospect of ever getting beyond a labouring job with a barrow and shovel. That lack of opportunity robbed them of ambition and aims for their future, with the result that the only exciting thing in the lives of many were the local gangs, the bottle stores and the locally grown marijuana. The drink and the drug often resulted in violent gang-warfare, with serious injury, arrests, court cases and imprisonment.

So my work was not just to teach in Sunday School! I needed to get out among these young people, visiting in their homes, playing, climbing, and organising camps. Also to speak at court cases where they were being tried and in some cases doing my best to get someone out of prison.

A number who attended the male adult class in the Sunday

School turned to the Lord Jesus and were converted. (Lady missionaries had a class for females in that group.) We had the joy of seeing a number of the gang members' lives transformed. The ladies also saw girls and women turning to the Lord Jesus for salvation.

Among those converted was a well known prostitute in the area. One Sunday morning she met one of the elderly ladies, a Mrs Crowie, who was on her way to the Sunday School. On asking Mrs Crowie where she was going, she laughed when told she was going to Sunday School. Mrs. Crowie then explained to her that there were classes for all ages in the Sunday School and she would be welcome to attend. To Mrs. Crowie's surprise, she accepted the invitation to go with her.

The other ladies in the class thought that she would never come back, but they were wrong. Not only did she cone back and attend regularly, but she was wonderfully converted by the grace of God. Her life was completely transformed, to the amazement of all who lived in the area. As the years went on, she became 'auntie' to the young Christians.

These converts began to feel the need of more opportunity for fellowship, worship and teaching than was possible in the large Sunday School which was made up of such varied ages. Also the hall in which we met on Sunday mornings was often in a filthy state as it was used during the week and late on Saturday nights for films, dances and other activities which meant that the state of the hall was not conducive to worship of the Lord.

It was felt that the time had come for us to 'plant' a church as a plot had become available. We would then be able to hold an evening service on Sunday for the converts and also to reach other families who did not come to the morning school in the hall. There was one difficulty, the plot had a very large hole in the middle where people had helped themselves to sand and soil for their gardens and local building work. In the end the hole proved to be a blessing in disguise. A line was stretched across to divide the hole and a competition organized between the boys and girls, who could get grown-ups to help them, to see which side could fill their half first.

There were sand dunes in the vicinity where sand and soil were available, so with buckets, barrows, horses and carts and a truck (paid for by the young people) the hole was soon filled. It was fun, and it increased the fellowship as it proved to be a good way to get to know one another better. Incidentally, the ladies' team won!

Until such times as we could arrange for the church to be built, we purchased a sectional hut for evening worship services. We still had to use the hall on Sunday mornings to accommodate the large Sunday School. But it was not very long before the hut was too small for the evening services as more and more people began to attend the worship and fellowship meetings. Former gang members brought their friends. This forced us to pray that the Lord would provide and enable us to get the church building erected.

When I approached an architect who was a member of a sectarian church and asked him to design a church to seat four hundred, he laughed and said, 'You are foolish.' (He did not know that I had agreed to be God's foolish donkey). He continued, 'You will have to sell the building as a cinema. It will be far too large for services in that area. You will never be able to gather enough people to fill it.' However, we went ahead with our plans, having faith that times of spiritual refreshing were coming from the Lord and that we were going to see many lost sheep coming into His 'fold'.

The Lord provided the money and the church was built. It was not very long, though, before the church was too small for those who attended and extensions had to be arranged. Today it is a large complex comprising the church and a number of halls and classrooms as a Missionary Training School is also located in the grounds. So the architect was wrong, for it now accommodates many more than the original estimated number.

More interesting still is the fact that six congregations, each with its own pastor, have grown out of that first congregation. When I have had the privilege to visit that part of South Africa in recent years, I have found that some of the old gang members who were converted over forty years ago are still active in the churches. I have been informed that during that period some have had perfect attendance for as many as twenty and thirty years! At the time of writing in 1995, my brother James and his family are based there. He is involved with the churches and is also principal of the Missionary School.

Of course, things have now changed in South Africa. Apartheid is unlawful, but it will take some time, however, for it to be eradicated from the minds of many who have lived for years under the culture of its influence, and those who controlled the system. But as far as the so called 'coloured' people are concerned, there have been opportunities for many years in the Cape, even before apartheid was removed from the statute-book, to receive secondary and university education.

In the above congregations now one can find ministers, doctors, lawyers, teachers and other graduates as well as very successful business men and women. One can see Mercedes cars at their houses, and large trolleys of groceries being wheeled from the supermarkets. Of course, there are many who are older and who are still suffering degrees of poverty, resulting, no doubt in many cases, from the lack of opportunities when they were younger.

I spent two and a half very happy years, from 1948 to 1951, in the Lord's work in that interesting part of His harvest field. I returned to Scotland in April that year where I was asked to take a temporary teaching post in the Missionary School where I trained. It was during that time in Scotland that I had to consider a particular problem that arose in my pastoral duties.

Isabel

I found it difficult, being single and still quite young, to have counselling sessions with young ladies. It was hard to discover what their motive was for asking to come and see me. Was it a genuine desire to receive spiritual help and advice, or was there a thought of winning my affection? Some might think that I was allowing my imagination to play too great a part. That might be so, but I certainly found it a barrier in my desire to win souls.

Before going back to Africa as I was planning to do, I felt I should get clear leading from the Lord on the question of marriage. I knew that I had promised the Lord that I was willing to remain single for the rest of my life if it was His will, but was it His will? After much prayer and waiting on the Lord for guidance, I felt led to approach the only young woman to whom I had felt drawn since returning from Africa. Although Isabel MacKenzie had already graduated, as part of further studies she was attending a class on Christian journalism which I was teaching.

I had a talk with the principal, sharing my feelings on the matter, and he thought that I was making a good choice. As we were no longer students and were exempt from the 'no contact between the male and female students' rule, I wrote Isabel a long eight-page letter. I tried to give her an idea of what would be involved in our lives together in Africa. By that time I had had a call to travel through a number of African countries, helping with special evangelistic services, conferences, elders' training and other matters on different mission stations. I wanted to be sure she knew what saying 'yes' to my proposal would mean! We began to go out together, talking and praying over the matter, and our understanding and love for each other grew, until we felt sure it was the Lord's will for us to marry.

Isabel's parents came from the Highlands of Scotland; her father from Lairg in Sutherland and her mother from Nairn near

Inverness. They met in Glasgow, where they were employed, got married and set up their home. Her home was also a Christian home where prayer and Bible reading took place in family worship. The church with its youth activities played a large part in her life.

Although she went faithfully to church for many years, she did not know that she could invite the Lord Jesus into her life personally. It was in her late teens, through the influence of her older sister who had found Jesus as her Saviour, that Isabel was introduced to Him, and received the assurance that her sins were forgiven.

Not very long after her conversion, she began to feel that God was calling her into full-time service. She asked the Lord the same question that Saul asked after his conversion, 'Lord, what do you want me to do?' She was guided to train as a nurse as the first step in preparing for missionary service, and was trained in Glasgow.

When her nurse's training was finished, she applied to the Metropolitan Missionary Training School where I had trained some years earlier. She knew some of the staff and students in the School, and her older sister was involved in public activities of the School. So Isabel decided that the type of Bible and practical training offered would be invaluable when the Lord opened the door for her to go to the mission field.

She never regretted that step, as during the years of her training she had wonderful opportunities for experience in evangelistic outreach and social work in needy areas of Glasgow and elsewhere at that time.

I had known Isabel for a short time before I left for South Africa in 1948 as I had a period of teaching in the Mission School in the mid-1940s while waiting for a passage. Isabel had arrived as a student and was in my class. Of course, I only knew her as a student! As mentioned, any other type of friendship would have been against the student rules.

But when I returned to Scotland after my two and a half years in South Africa the situation was different. Her training was already finished and so she was no longer a student. That is why I was able to correspond with her and we were able to discuss and pray together over the Lord's plan for our future.

I understand that when Isabel found my long letter in her mail box it came as a great surprise to her! Entirely unknown to me but known to all the other ladies, there was another young woman among the postgraduate students who was expecting me to propose to her! That is why Isabel did not expect such a sudden development, but she tells me she was not sorry that the proposal came her way. However, we felt the need of getting to know each other better as our contacts up to that time had only been 'official' .

Isabel told me that, after our discussions and prayers together during the weeks that followed, she had the assurance that it was the Lord's will for her to accept my proposal. How glad I was to hear her say 'Yes.' I have never regretted sending her the letter and she says she has never regretted saying, 'yes'. She still has the eight-page letter, after forty-three years of marriage!

Here are two paragraphs which she has written expressing her feelings at that time:

'Jack, who had been one of my teachers in the school before he left for Africa, returned to Scotland after his first term of service. With my call to missionary work we had much in common, as we got better acquainted with each other, no longer under "student rules". However, he was apprehensive about asking me to be his wife. He thought that the type of itinerant missionary work to which he felt called would be too strenuous for me, so he decided to put these difficulties into an eight-page letter which he wrote to me! If I felt I could accept them, then his letter was a proposal! After praying and discussing together during the following weeks, I had the assurance that it was the Lord's will for me to accept the proposal. I have never regretted making that decision. I still have the eight-page letter, after forty-three years!

'We were married in November 1952 and that was the beginning of a very interesting life with Jack. We were only married about two weeks when he had to leave for an area in Africa where it was not permissible for a woman to travel, because of political unrest. I remained in Scotland and did not see him again for ten months, until I arrived in Mombasa in September 1953.'

4

Kenya

As Isabel has mentioned I sailed for Africa again in December, 1952. I was going to Kenya which had become notorious for its violence and political unrest because of the Mau Mau uprising. It was not advisable for women to travel in the area at that time unless it was absolutely necessary, so I was not allowed to take Isabel with me while I would be travelling there.

My commission was to visit mission work in nine of the African countries on behalf of the Bible School in Glasgow, with a twofold purpose in view. First, to try to be an encouragement to missionaries and local Christians in isolated areas, and secondly to provide for the Bible School a clearer view of the missionary situation. The journey was to commence in Mombasa, Kenya and end in Cape Town, South Africa.

The violence of the Mau Mau uprising was gaining momentum by the time we landed in Mombasa on the 31st of December that year after twenty-six days at sea. We sailed through the Mediterranean, the Suez canal and the Red Sea.

I was thankful that the Bible School had arranged for me to have a companion with me in my travels until Isabel could join me. Willie Webster from Glasgow, who had been a mature student in the Bible School, was appointed to travel with me. He proved to be a wonderful companion. But of course, I did miss my dear Isabel very much. It had been such a short time between our wedding and my departure. Before I left we had arranged to meet in prayer each evening at 9.00 pm British time when possible. That was the closest we could get together under the circumstances.

My thoughts were often back in Scotland, wondering what Isabel was doing – was she missing me? How long would it be before we would see each other again? Was it possible that I might never see her again because of the dangers that surrounded our journey in Africa? I can only leave the reader to imagine some of the feelings which left an aching void in the heart when separated at such a distance from the one I loved most in the world.

But to get back to our landing in Mombasa: it was quite a wonderful experience for Willie and me. Here is part of a letter that Willie wrote to his friends, describing some of his first impressions:

'I feel a little bit like a wee fellow who goes for the first time to the zoo, with his eyes wide open and eagerly asking many questions. We landed in Mombasa just after lunch on New Year's Eve. The heat was terrific, colour seemed everywhere, so different from our twenty-six days on the ship, surrounded by water.

'I know this is the beginning of a great adventure, and I don't feel equal to it. But when one knows that God has sent him he feels like an ambassador with credentials of a high order.'

It was very amusing after we arrived at the Mission Guest House in Mombasa to hear from a party next door, the words of the song, 'I belang to Glasga'. Willie, being a Glasgow man, was quite amused to hear a song about his city when he was thousands of miles from home!

When we left Mombasa we travelled over rough and dusty roads in the small van which we brought with us on the ship. In another of Willie's letters, he described these travelling conditions:

'On we go now, over roads covered with fine sand, the colour of light cocoa. It gets into the van and sticks to everything. Jack has to keep his eyes on the road as there are some very bad potholes which give the van some terrible jolts.'

But there were more than potholes that had to be avoided! On our trip from Mombasa to Nairobi we saw a large elephant on the road ahead of us. As we approached, it walked into the bushes at the side of the road. We decided to stop for a photo. It was standing a few yards from the road looking at us. Suddenly it began to look ferocious and to toss up soil with its tusks, and we realised that it was about to charge us. Her calf was in the bushes on the opposite side of the road and we had separated them, hence her anger. I took a photo quickly and drove off. When the film was developed, there was no elephant on the print – the photographer was too nervous to aim correctly.

First Tooth Extraction
Another unusual thing happened during our first days in Kenya. We had been camping for the night when I saw Willie coming across the grass carrying a four-gallon petrol can, followed by an elderly woman who was holding her jaw. Putting down the can and seating the woman on it, he said, 'Jack, this woman has a very painful tooth. Pull it out.'

Willie knew that my dentist in Glasgow had given me some forceps and a few tips on how to extract a tooth, but I had never done an extraction. When I saw the size of the large molar tooth and its decayed condition, I told Willie that I was reluctant to attempt to extract it, 'Come on, Jack, give it a try, she is in very severe pain,' he said as he walked away.

There was not much else for me to do but try. I knew that we were very far away from any place where she could get proper dental treatment. Producing the forceps I realised that I was more nervous than the patient, although she was not going to have any anaesthetic. With prayer and trembling hands, the tooth came out without one murmur from the lady.

With the tooth in the forceps, I called Willie to show him that I had succeeded, but although I called loudly there was no reply. I could not understand where he had gone as we were camping in a small area. I thought he would be interested to see if I had managed the extraction as he was the one who had introduced the patient! I went off to try and find him, with the tooth in the forceps to show him that I had succeeded. I found him sitting in our tent with his fingers pressed into his ears. I asked him what was wrong. 'I did not want to hear the woman screaming,' was his reply.

That was not the last tooth I extracted. It was the first of many hundreds, but only after I had taken a course in medicine and dentistry in the Missionary School of Medicine in London in the 1960s. After a number of years in Africa, I realised what General Booth of the Salvation Army meant when he said, 'There is no point in preaching to a person who has toothache.'

Martyrs for Jesus
Our first calls were in the area of unrest caused by the Mau Mau uprising. The initiation into the Mau Mau was linked to a witchcraft oath which required members, among other things, not to support the church in any way, by contributing, attending, or having their children baptised. The oath, which members were forced to take, also required the promise that they would be willing to bring in the head of a white person, if asked to do so. The oath was confirmed with the drinking of sheep's blood and the statement, 'If I break this oath, let it kill me.' Because of their fear of witchcraft in most cases, they believed that they would die if they broke the promise.

The oath was forced on people, and anyone who refused to be initiated was threatened with death. Many Christians died rather than deny Jesus. One Christian said, 'When the Mau Mau knock comes to your door at night, either Jesus means everything to you, or nothing at all.' There were many reports of the great joy given by God when they faced death.

During the period before this uprising there had been a wonderful movement of the Holy Spirit in East Africa. The revival commenced in Rwanda and spread through Uganda to Kenya. It resulted in deep conviction for sin, causing many to come to the Lord for forgiveness and cleansing. Many of the churches were greatly blessed by the revival, especially in the Kikuyu tribal area where the Presbyterian Church of East Africa was very strong. Many had found new life in Christ. It was wonderful how the Lord had prepared His people in that area for the time of persecution which was to follow, especially as the Mau Mau uprising commenced in Kikuyuland.

When the Mau Mau launched the uprising, the church members became the target of very cruel persecution because they were unwilling to take the occult oath which required the denial of Christ and His church. That infuriated the leaders of Mau Mau as they felt that the Christian faith was a large barrier to their success in forcing the British Government to give the country independence. Notices were found on church doors stating that anyone who attended church would be killed. One denomination which was not too keen to welcome the revival, as the Presbyterians had done, reported that they had lost 96% of their membership. Through fear they stopped attending the services.

Willie and I had the joy of meeting many Christians and sharing in their fellowship meetings. Our main purpose in being in the area was to seek, by God's help, to encourage the Christians in their stand for Christ, but seeing their faith and joy we received much more blessing and inspiration than we could ever have given them. Let me share a few illustrations of their wonderful faith, joy and devotion to Christ which we discovered while we were there.

We were taken one day to a grave beside a church. It was the grave of Miriam, a young mother who had been killed by the Mau Mau. The Christians who were with us explained what had happened to her. With a baby on her back, she and an older woman were walking in the forest. The Mau Mau gang, recognising Miriam as a Christian by the way she was dressed, challenged her to deny Christ by giving up her faith and promising not to attend church any more. When she refused, they snatched the baby from her back, threw it to the older woman, and murdered her.

After preaching at Chogoria where Rev. Dr. Clive Irvine, a Church of Scotland missionary, was in charge of the station, he introduced me to a lay preacher who was in the congregation. I noticed that his head was very badly scarred. The preacher then told me that one day he received a letter which had been sent from the Mau Mau ordering him to stop preaching about Jesus or he would be killed. Like Peter and John who were told not to preach any more about Jesus, he said to me, 'How could I stop preaching about Jesus because of such threats, when He meant so much to me. I just carried on preaching, ignoring their letter.' Then he told how one day, after he had preached in a school room to a number who were willing to disobey the Mau Mau and attend the service, a gang was waiting for him in the bushes as he left the building.

With a large knife, called a 'panga' in the local language but very similar to a butcher's chopping knife, they chopped his skull and left, after setting fire to the thatch on the school roof, thinking he was dead. He was found by some villagers who came to investigate the fire, and they took him to the Mission hospital at Chogoria. Clive Irvine, as well as being a doctor of divinity, was also a medical doctor. He told me that when the preacher was brought to the hospital he held out very little hope for his recovery because his brain was exposed. But he called the African minister on the station and together they prayed that if it was the Lord's will, he would recover. Clive then operated.

In one month he had recovered so well, without any permanent damage to his brain, that Clive decided he could be discharged, although he would have to wear bandages for a time. The doctor considered his recovery a divine miracle. When the patient told his relatives that he could go home, they asked him where he wanted to hide as the Mau Mau thought they had killed him. He told his relatives, 'I am not going to hide. Jesus is my Saviour, and He is my best Friend, so I am not going to run away from the work He has given me to do. Satan is trying to frighten me out of God's service!'

He went back to the villages and continued to preach, and he was never attacked again. Perhaps his superstitious attackers thought that he had risen from the dead! But when I saw him, he was still carrying the scars which he had received on his head, the badges of his love and devotion for the defence of his Lord and Master. What faithfulness!

One night Willie and I were staying in the home of a government doctor when he was called out by the police. They wanted him to confirm the cause of the death of an elderly woman whose body had been found in a shallow grave. When the doctor returned he told us a sad, but touching story. He said that, according to the police report, the elderly woman whose body had been buried had been walking in the forest with four other women when they were ambushed by a gang.

The gang took them to a hut where they were asked to take the Mau Mau oath. They were all church members, but unfortunately four of them were afraid and agreed to take the oath. But the elderly woman refused. She said, 'I have taken Holy Communion where the cup I have been given represents the blood of the Lord Jesus and I can never drink this animal blood and promise to keep the oath.'

They threatened her with death if she refused to drink the

blood, but she informed them that if they killed her, she would just go to be with Jesus as He was the one she loved. They left some of the gang to guard the other women. (I expect it was one of them who later gave the report that the police received.) The other members of the gang marched the old woman two miles into the forest, murdered her there and buried her in the shallow grave. I have often thought of the courage, strength and joy which the Lord must have given her as she walked the two miles. Anywhere along the way she could have changed her mind and recanted, as she knew what was waiting for her at the end.

She could have allowed fear to overcome her, but the Lord must have given her the joy of His presence, as Stephen experienced in Acts 6:15 when we read that the council, 'saw his face as it had been the face of an angel', and he prayed for his murderers as they stoned him. It is sad that only her murderers were with her at the end. It would have been very interesting to have an account of how she faced her murderers and the testimony she must have given them.

A minister and his wife, sleeping in a little thatched manse, woke up one night with the smell of smoke. The thatch was on fire. Rushing outside, they found the gang who had set fire to the thatch waiting for them. The minister was challenged and asked to promise to give up his work for the church and take the oath. He refused. He gave the same reason as many others who had died, 'The Lord Jesus has saved me and forgiven me. I love Him. He is my best Friend and I cannot forsake Him now.'

He and his wife were taken deeper into the forest. One end of a rope was tied round his neck and the other thrown over the branch of a tree. He was then pulled up off the ground, but not 'hung' with a drop. As he was hanging there he became unconscious. He was then taken down and cold water poured over him until he regained consciousness. He was given another opportunity to recant, but he said, 'I have already given you my answer.'

Three times they repeated this cruel act and each time he gave the same answer, but after the fourth time they could not revive him again. He had gone to be with his heavenly Saviour and Friend. What a wonderful reception such martyrs must get when they reach the other side!

His wife had to watch her husband die. Then the gang turned to her and said, 'What is your answer?' 'It is the same as my husband's answer,' she said. The gang then informed her that, as it was almost dawn and they were afraid of being found by the police, they would lock her up for the day and she would meet the same fate as her husband when darkness came. But she escaped during the day and was able to tell the story of the triumphant but cruel death of her husband.

A Christian farmer's home and steading were attacked one night by a Mau Mau gang. They burned his home and farm buildings and drove away all his animals. Some of his Christian friends arrived the next morning to do what they could to support him in his great loss. They found him sitting on the ground, near his burned out buildings, repeating Scripture from Habakkuk 3:17, 18: 'The flock shall be cut off from the fold, and there shall be no herd in the stalls; yet I will rejoice in the Lord, I will joy in the God of my salvation.'

It is only 'the joy of the Lord' that gives strength on such occasions of loss or suffering, as Nehemiah points out. Those months in Kenya, at the time when the Christians were facing such severe trials of suffering and cruel death, are months that I shall never forget. It seemed as if we were back in the time of the Acts of the Apostles, and the first three-hundred year period of the young Church when it suffered such hatred and martyrdom. But as the 'blood of the martyrs was the seed of the church' then, causing it to grow in those early years, so it was in Kenya. The church was cleansed from the love of worldly things, knowing that at any moment the Mau Mau knock could come to the door and then it was only their relationship with Jesus that mattered!

We visited other mission stations in Kenya, and had the opportunity of ministering. We had the privilege of working with missionaries and ministers of the Africa Inland Mission, the Church Missionary Society, and the Londiana Industrial Mission before going to Uganda.

5

Uganda

The plan had been that when we had ended our calls in Kenya, I should go on into Uganda. I had expected Isabel to join me by air at the end of the trip in Kenya, as Willie was only to accompany me in the restricted area of Kenya where it was dangerous for Isabel to travel. However, when we reached Uganda, I was informed from headquarters that the plan had changed. Isabel would not be arriving meantime and Willie was to stay with me until further notice.

It hurt me to think of how Isabel must have felt when she was told that her trip was postponed. I knew how much she had been looking forward to our reunion. I found myself carrying her disappointment as well as my own. But I could not allow those intense feelings of disappointment to cloud the time in Uganda and distract us from the work the Lord wanted us to do there.

Of course, I still appreciated Willie's companionship. He was a very good friend and I was so glad of his help and fellowship. In fact, I may owe my life to him. When we were crossing the equator at a very isolated spot before leaving Kenya, we decided to camp for a few days of rest. While there I had a very serious attack of food poisoning. I had never remembered being so ill. We were far away from any help and Willie could not drive the vehicle. He nursed me with great care until eventually he was able to stop a lady motorist. He explained my position and brought her into the little tent where I was lying.

She was the wife of a farmer and lived some miles away. I think she was a trained nurse, but anyway she took over the situation and arranged for me to get treatment. Later, when I recovered, we were invited to her home for a meal.

An invasion in our tent

While we were still camping, in the middle of a night we were invaded by a colony of stinging ants! We had left our little water filter tap dripping, and word was taken back to the anthill by one of their scouts that there was water in the tent, hence the invasion. But they were not satisfied with water, they wanted to add some flesh. As I was lying on a mattress on the ground and Willie was on a camp bed, I was more easily available. I awoke with the pain of their bites and found dozens of them inside my pyjamas. Jumping off the mattress and flailing my arms to knock off the ants, I woke up Willie. He admitted afterwards that his first reaction was to conclude that I was delirious! We did not leave the tap dripping again!

In Uganda we found many lonely and overworked missionaries, pastors and lay preachers in out-of-the-way mission stations and church centres. We received very warm and enthusiastic receptions from them and many requests to change our plans and stay longer.

The Rwanda Revival

We saw much evidence of the effects of the 'Rwanda Revival' in Uganda. Wherever we went fellowship meetings were being held in churches, schools and often in homes. Men and women gathered together to sing, pray and praise the Lord and to share their testimonies. They were very open about their Christian experiences, and those who felt they had grieved the Lord in any way since they had last met would bring the matter 'out to the light', to use their expression. A basic text often quoted in the fellowship meetings was 1 John 1:7: 'If we walk in the light, as He is in the light, we have fellowship one with another, and the blood of Jesus Christ His Son cleanseth us from all sin.' One could liken these meetings to the original class meetings of the early Methodists when the converts met to share their spiritual lives, and to get advice and warnings from the older Christians.

Weaknesses connected to the revival

I must admit that sometimes, if there was not good leadership, I felt that there were weak spots in the fellowships, although one had to be careful not to be critical. I thought that some of the confessions made in the fellowships were not appropriate for public airing when they dealt with intimate matters between husbands and wives, or when another person was implicated. Occasionally the meetings could drift into long periods of confessing failures and very few accounts of victories. In fact, sometimes when victory was mentioned it was looked upon as spiritual pride, while confession of failure was looked upon as humility, which caused a rather dangerous precedent. The fact that failure could be confessed at the next meeting dampened the desire for a victorious life, it seemed.

As an example, one day after a fellowship meeting, the minister who had led it asked if he could have a chat with me. He then told me that he was now very disappointed with the state into which his fellowship had drifted. He said that there used to be many young people who attended the meeting, but now it was only made up of elderly people. I pointed out to him that the longest session in the meeting was given to people who poured out their temptations, weaknesses and failures, and admitting that they had yielded to them. There were no testimonies to the grace and power of God enabling people to overcome sin which Paul tells us should not have dominion over us! There were only short periods of singing, reading the Scripture and praying.

I said to the minister, 'I can see how young people would soon get discouraged by attending these meetings. If elderly professing Christians can only report failure during most of the meeting, and there are no testimonies to inspire them to a life of joyfully walking with Jesus in a path of overcoming, and no Scripture teaching to encourage them to live such a life, they would only go home depressed with little desire to return.'

Notable converts of the revival

However, there were many hundreds of lives changed as a result of the testimonies of those who had been revived. Two of the wonderful products of the revival in Uganda were William Nagenda and Festo Kivengere who became well known worldwide for their reviving ministry. Isabel and I had the privilege of knowing them personally in later years. I had been invited to speak at a conference for Christians in Zambia in 1961, to which William and Festo had also been invited as speakers. We had wonderful fellowship together.

It so happened that during the conference Isabel had been flown over to hospital in Zambia as she had been having complications with her pregnancy, and the local doctor in Malawi refused to take responsibility for the delivery of the baby. He wanted her to have specialist attention. When William and Festo heard about Isabel's difficulties, they both decided to visit the hospital, although they were very busy with services and sessions of counselling. They had special prayer with her and for the safe delivery of the baby. What loving concern they had. There was much praising of the Lord a few days later when baby Ruth arrived.

We did not know William as well as we knew Festo. I met William once in Uganda in 1953, and the time we were at the conference in Zambia was the only other time that we shared together. There is a lovely story told about William, and I would like to pass it on to show his love and devotion to Jesus.

He was on a mission station for a few days visiting the missionaries when a lady doctor of anthropology arrived to spend a few days doing research on the station. William asked the missionary in charge of the station, 'Is that doctor a Christian?'

'I don't know,' the missionary replied, 'I have not found out.' William was not happy to leave things like that, so the first opportunity he found, he asked her, 'Do you read the Bible?'

'Oh no,' she said, 'The Bible is a very dry and uninteresting book to me.' William then said to her, 'May I tell you a little story?'

'Of course,' she said. He then told her about a young woman who bought a book, the title of which looked quite attractive, but when she started reading it she found it very uninteresting and left it unread on the bookshelf. Sometime later she met a young man and they fell in love and began to go out together. One evening in their conversation, she discovered that the young man was the author of the book she had bought sometime before! When she went home that night she searched for the book and did not stop reading until she reached the end!

All that William further said to her before he left was, 'Doctor, it makes a great difference to a book when you know the Author.'

William was later invited to England when he needed specialist treatment and he had a wonderful testimony among university students. He remained there until the time of his death.

We knew Festo better than we knew William as we were together at other conferences. He was a very effective evangelist, with a special ministry to students. I had the privilege in the early 1970s to help to arrange a pastor's conference in Malawi for him and the late Dr. Paul Rees of World Vision. Isabel and I knew him personally and he had a strong influence on our lives spiritually. Festo being on Idi Amin's deathlist had to flee from Uganda. He too has now gone to his heavenly home.

But I have wandered away from Uganda with these stories of two of her sons who accomplished much for the kingdom of God – fruit of what has been called the Rwanda Revival.

Handymen

Willie and I spent another three months travelling through Uganda. As well as the spiritual aspects of our visits to mission stations, we were often engaged as handymen! I had such jobs as taking a pedal organ to pieces to find out why most of the notes played at once as soon as the missionary's wife began to pedal! I found that insects had built little nests of clay under the reeds which kept them all open. Another time it was to empty a delivery room in a hospital of a swarm of bees. Sometimes it was oil pressure lamps that would not work, or if there was a generator, searching for an electrical fault. Willie, having been a joiner, could find plenty to do on the stations with faulty wood-work. The problems mostly arose if there was no male missionary on the station.

In May, 1953 we decided to travel to the West Nile district of Uganda. That was a part of Uganda in the north which lay west of the Nile. The Africa Inland Mission had centres there, although in an unusual arrangement the missionaries came under the wing of the Anglican Church Missionary Society in Uganda. Responsibility for all non-Catholic missions in the country needed CMS permission at that time.

We had an unusual happening before we crossed the Nile on a ferry. We were to call at a mission station on the way but were having difficulty in finding it. We tried to stop two African young men who were approaching us on bicycles to ask the way to the mission station. They jumped off their bicycles, threw them down on the road, and ran into the bushes. Nothing we could do was able to entice them back.

Afterwards when we found the mission station, we asked the missionary why the young men would act in that way. Did they think we were police? He smiled and said, 'No! It is Black Boy Meat.' He then told us that an overseas' firm decided to market some tinned meat especially for Africa. The tin was labelled 'Black Boy Meat' and had a photo of an African on the label. When the tins appeared on the shelves in the little village shops, they were placed beside tins with fish, cows and sheep on the labels. It did not take the villagers long to come to the conclusion that if the other tins contained flesh of fish, cows and sheep, the one with the African on the label must contain meat from the bodies of black boys!

The missionary went on to tell us that when the meat arrived, it did not take long for the lines of the 'bush telegraph' to get hot as the message was passed from village to village that white men were coming round in vans and collecting boys for tinning. The missionary said, 'Your van is the type in which it is said that boys are collected. A white man was killed in his van one night when it broke down. A mob attacked the van and killed him, thinking he was waiting for the morning, so that he could round up some boys!'

At the time Willie and I were stunned by the foolishness of the firm that put such a label on their meat, but we did not give it much more thought as we continued our travels. However, one night a few months later, when I was alone in the Belgian Congo and surrounded by a mob, memory of the account the missionary had given us flashed into my mind! I will explain that incident later.

After leaving the mission station mentioned above Willie and I were on our way to cross the Nile and reach a leprosarium of the Africa Inland Mission called Kuluva, which was supervised by two brothers, Doctors Ted and Peter Williams.

Ted told me an interesting story of how the hospital came to be located in that place. The international headquarters of the Mission had decided that it should be built in the town of Arua near the Zaire border; but as there was a general hospital already in the vicinity of the town, Ted decided that Arua was not the right place. He felt that the hospital should be out in a rural area where no other medical facilities were available. He then did as Nehemiah did before he started building the walls of Jerusalem, he went out to have a look around the area without telling the leaders. Ted surveyed the district and found the place where the hospital is now situated. He decided that it was the spot where they should build. The local chief was in favour and they came to an agreement.

Ted then sent a cable to his headquarters in England. The cable only contained the Scripture reference: 'Nehemiah chapter two, verse sixteen.' When his committee turned to the verse, they read, 'The rulers knew not whither I went or what I did.' The committee finally gave their permission to build on the plot he had chosen!

We were accommodated by Ted and his wife Muriel which made a great change from the confined space of the van. Our sleeping part of the small van had a floor space which was only four and a half feet by six feet, and the height was four and a half feet. When we turned in our bunks, which were built above cupboards, our elbows would scrape the ceiling of the van. The fact that we were not sleeping in the van while with the Williams, allowed Willie to put his joinery skill into practice, and he reduced the wooden cupboards so that our bunks were lowered.

We had received word that a passage was being sought for Isabel to sail to Mombasa and once the date was settled, Willie was to fly home to Scotland. Because we had to wait for this information, we felt it best not to move since once we started travelling we 'were of no fixed abode' and mail could take a long time to reach us.

We were with the Williams on Coronation Day which was a holiday. I decided to take a short trip to see another part of the area and Muriel played a trick on me when she packed a picnic lunch. When I was enjoying it around noon that day, I thought the meat pies had an unfamiliar flavour so I decided to take the top off one to investigate. I found roasted termite ants with their heads and legs sticking out! I knew that the Africans looked upon these roasted ants as a delicacy, but I had never tried to eat them. I must admit that I liked the taste of them, but after seeing them I did not eat any more! Missionary humour on Muriel's part, but she was not giving me something that she and Ted would not eat. They kept a bowl of roasted ants on the dining room table and ate them like we would eat roasted nuts.

At the end of June, Willie was asked to fly back to Scotland and I was informed that Isabel would sail in July from Southampton through the Suez Canal and the Red Sea to Mombasa, a journey of about six weeks. I knew that I would miss Willie who had been such a good friend and companion. His hallelujahs and praises to the Lord had not allowed us to become too discouraged or depressed!

I was overjoyed, of course, that Isabel and I would soon be together again, although August did seem to be more distant than I would have liked.

6

Zaire

As I had a number of weeks to wait between the time Willie left and Isabel was due to arrive, I felt led by the Lord to cross into what is now Zaire. My first night in the country was to be a memorable one!

The day had been very trying, as I had to drive over corrugated clay and gravel roads with many potholes on what to me was the wrong side of the road. Traffic travels on the right hand side of the road in Zaire – no easy job when the steering wheel is still located in the position to drive on the left hand side. I only found out then how many things I did automatically when driving on the left side, and had difficulty adjusting my 'automatic pilot'.

As the sun was just about to set in all its tropical glory behind a range of mountains, I felt that I should try to find a place where I could camp and rest for the weekend as it was Friday. I was heading for a very large Africa Inland Mission station called Rethy, and I expected that there would be a number of requests for me to speak on Sunday as there was a church, secondary school, nurses' training school and also a school for missionaries' children on the station. I felt that it would be good to have a weekend break before engaging in such activities. Little did I realise that it would be one of the most unforgettable weekends of my life!

I was preparing to retire to my bunk late in the evening, amid all the noises of an African night. Frogs, crickets, birds and myriads of insects all combined in their nocturnal chorus, to the accompaniment of tom-tom drums in the distant villages.

Then suddenly, all around the van, wild shouts and screams announced that I had been surrounded by a mob. Into my mind immediately, with alarming concern, flashed the story of BLACK BOY MEAT, about which I had been told by the missionary in Uganda!

In the midst of our travels I had forgotten about the information on 'Black Boy Meat', but there in my lonely camping spot, surrounded by the screaming mob, I remembered and trembled! I peered out through a gap in the curtain and saw the spears glistening in the moonlight, and my trembling increased.

Then I had a very strange experience. I was conscious that the Lord was asking me a question, not with an audible voice, but I felt Him speaking internally. The question was: 'Who sent you here?'

'I am here on Your business and because You sent me!' I secretly answered.

'Don't you think that I can look after you then?' came the Lord's assurance.

That assurance helped me to realise that no-one could touch me unless the Lord allowed them to do so. Immediately my trembling stopped, and hardly realising what I was doing, I opened the window, put out my head and greeted them. At once the shouting and screaming stopped, and there was complete silence for a few seconds as I had taken them by surprise. Then they began to ask many questions: 'From where do you come?' 'Where are you going?' 'What are you doing here?'

As I had just arrived in Zaire, I did not know any of the local language. Whether I received the gift of 'another tongue' or not I don't know, but with scraps of other languages I had picked up, the Lord helped me to explain that I was a missionary and that I was on my way to Rethy mission station. They knew the mission station because there was a large hospital where they received treatment when they were ill. Eventually they seemed to be persuaded that I was not there to catch black boys for tinning and their questions stopped. I then said goodbye to them, pulled my head back into the van and closed the window, hoping they would take the hint and go away. I could still hear some movement around the van for a short time, but eventually it stopped. Being very tired, I dropped off into a troubled sleep – but not for long!

My van was surrounded again about 2.30 am by shouting and blood curdling screeches rending the air. Waking up in a strange place always has its few seconds of daze, trying to find one's position, but I was roused to consciousness very quickly, and to the memories of Black Boy Meat!

Concluding that I had been discovered by a different group of people, going home perhaps from a midnight 'beer drinking' party, I thought it better to refrain from putting my head out into the night. Many thoughts rushed through my mind in the next few moments. The ignorant decision of a meat firm, thousands of miles away, to use such a foolish name for their product had brought me within a few inches, and perhaps a few seconds of death. Would word reach my bride in Scotland that she was a widow, although we had only lived together for a few days?

As my thoughts raced on, the noise outside gained momentum, and I realised that an attack was imminent. Time was running out, and if I wanted to stave off the attack I had to act at once. I shouted greetings from my bunk with the help of what languages I could muster. The noise began to subside and I repeated the greeting, in case, owing to the noise, some had not heard me. That resulted in a lull in the noise, and I shouted, 'I am a missionary on my way to Rethy mission station and I am just resting.'

I could hear the name of the mission station being repeated as they discussed whether to accept my story or not. Eventually they seemed to come to the conclusion that they should wait. I found out later that they had decided to wait until sunrise to verify my explanation. I could hear their voices trailing off into the night as they withdrew from the van.

I was alone again, as far as I could gather, but not in any mood to sleep! I decided that if I was still alive in the morning I would be off at the crack of dawn. Gradually the blackness of the tropical night began to give way to the approaching grey of dawn, and as the sun rises very quickly over the horizon when one is close to the equator, it was not long before daylight had come.

I peered out each of the little windows in the van to see if I was under siege, and as I could not see anyone I decided to try to make a quick getaway. But as I had left some of my cooking and other equipment outside the van during the night to give me more space inside, I had to go out of the van to collect it. When I opened the back door and stepped out, I got a shock. I was confronted by two large men who were standing like sentries in a position where I could not see them from a window.

I tried to shake hands with them and greet them, but they refused my greeting, which is very unusual with Africans, and I wondered what was going to happen to me. They pushed past me and looked very intently into the van. Suddenly their faces relaxed, and with smiles they held out their hands and returned my greeting. They had seen no evidence of captured boys or tinned meat in the van!

They walked off into the forest and I thought that was my time to rush off. But before I could pack and get the van started, I saw them returning at the head of a column of about thirty villagers. It seemed the group had been concealed in the bushes waiting to hear the report of the two men. If they had seen anything suspicious which they thought would have proved that I was involved in collecting boys, they would have called them out for an attack, and I expect my earthly journey would have ended there. But instead, because they had seemed to believe the explanation that I was a missionary, they produced a basin of eggs for me, and stood around in a circle as they presented it. What an anticlimax!

After such a gift and warm reception, I decided to remain for the weekend as at first planned, because I now felt safe. So I set up my little folding table and chair, lit the primus stove, and fried two of the eggs they had brought. They were amused to see fire without wood, but they were much more amused to see me eating the fried eggs with a knife and fork instead of using my fingers as they do. They seemed to think it was very funny, as they stood around me in a circle, nudging one another with their elbows and bursting with laughter. All I could think of was the monkeys' tea party at a zoo, and I was the monkey!

However, later that morning, a Belgian Government official arrived in his large American car. He informed me that it had been reported to the police that a white man was lost in the bush, so he had come to find out the position. Some African must have concluded from the meetings in the night, my language being limited, that I was lost and did not know how to proceed to the mission station. I explained my reason to the official, informing him that I was a missionary, but being quite tired, I wanted to take the weekend to rest. He understood, but was not happy to leave me there. He said it was dangerous because of the local situation. I told him how the local people had received me and I felt quite safe and would like to stay.

The local people told him that they wanted me to stay and that they would bring me water and anything else I needed, like firewood. He then told me that if I wanted to stay he would not force me to move, so he left me. But later in the afternoon, an African soldier rode up on a bicycle and, after giving me an elaborate salute, presented me with a letter from the official. The letter informed me that my position had been discussed at the local government headquarters and it was decided that I should not remain in my isolated situation.

The letter also extended an invitation to spend the weekend

in the home of the official. Of course, I then had to move, to the disappointment of the local villagers, but they had seen the soldier and knew that it was government orders. I spent a restful and comfortable weekend as his guest, although his wife was away at the time in Belgium and he was managing on his own, with the help of his African servants.

On the Monday I proceeded to the mission station where I had the joy of fellowship with the missionaries and local Christians and gave talks to groups of nurses and secondary school students. I was interested while there to meet one of the missionaries who was related to the late John Stam. John and his wife Betty were missionaries in China where they were executed for their faith.

I had many other interesting visits to churches, hospitals, schools and a leprosarium. I visited mission areas of the Africa Inland Mission, The Unevangelised Fields' Mission, and The Worldwide Evangelisation Crusade (known as the Heart of Africa Mission in Zaire when founded by C. T. Studd). But I did not know that seven years later a floodtide of cruel persecution was to burst on the church there when the Belgian Government withdrew from the country and independence was declared.

That uprising in the early 1960s was known as the Simba Rebellion. (Simba is a local language word for lion.) The rebellion started as an army mutiny against the newly independent government, because it did not, and could not, fulfil wild promises of riches, white peoples' houses, cars and even their wives, which politicians had made to the electorate before the elections.

It seemed quite clear that communistic influences fanned the flame of rebellion, and with the usual communistic atheistic opposition to religion, the rebellion spread to the local Christians and missionaries. Dr. Helen Roseveare has described in her books some of the awful atrocities that took place, as she was a missionary doctor there during that time and was one of those who suffered severely. Local church leaders and Christians were beaten and killed. Missionaries were imprisoned, raped and shot.

Isabel had a nephew, Billy Dalby who, with his wife and family, was a missionary there at that time. About 3.30 in the morning a message reached them that the Simbas were on their way and that they should get to a local airfield quickly where a plane was waiting. As they travelled on the back of a lorry closed in by a canvas covering they were ambushed by the Simbas. Billy found an old brush handle lying in the lorry and he stuck it out under the canvas. The Simbas scattered, thinking it was a gun, and the family escaped and reached the plane safely.

Apolo

In Zaire I had the privilege of standing at the grave of an African called Apolo who had gone over to Zaire from Uganda to preach the gospel to a tribe of Pygmies who live in the Ituri Forest – known at that time as the largest rain forest in the world. Apolo was a convert of the early Scottish missionary, Alexander MacKay of Uganda, and he took the name of Apolo as a Christian name.

After his conversion he informed his friends that he intended to cross over the mountains to Zaire to tell the Pygmies about Jesus. They tried to persuade him to give up the idea as it was too dangerous. The Pygmies were known to be experts with their little bows and poisoned arrows. But his call from God was so strong, he packed his few belongings and took the long journey on foot over what were known as the 'mountains of the moon'. As far as I know he was the first 'missionary' to enter that country with the gospel.

At first the small people were frightened and climbed up the trees to get away from him, but soon he won their confidence and a number of them were converted. That upset the witch-doctors as people were losing confidence in them, so they demanded that the chief must send Apolo back to Uganda. The chief, being afraid of the witchdoctors, ordered him to go, but Apolo refused. He said that God had sent him there and he could not run away. The witchdoctors then arranged that he should be tied to a tree and beaten to death.

Thinking that he was dead, they threw him into the forest so that the wild animals would eat his body, but an old woman who had been converted, decided to bury him secretly during the night. To her surprise she discovered that he was not dead, although he was unconscious. She decided to keep that a secret and to drag him into an area where it was not likely that people would find him. There she built a little hut over him, and when he regained consciousness she took food to him, although he was in great pain from the awful beating.

After three months he was able to walk a little around the trees. Then one day he announced to the old woman that early the next morning he would be going back into the village. She did her best to stop him, telling him that the witchdoctors thought he was dead, and that he should leave secretly for Uganda at night. But the next morning, he started off for the village and arrived before dawn at the little church which he had built. He began to beat the drum which was still hanging at the church door. The village had a great shock, as the drum had never sounded from the day Apolo was 'killed', as they thought.

Soon the cry went around the village that Apolo was back. It seemed as if his opponents thought he had risen from the dead! He was not molested again, but was left free to continue to preach the gospel until the time of his death. How inspiring it was to stand by his grave and reflect on his great love for his Lord and his devotion to Him in spite of great opposition.

One day as I was on my way out of Zaire, I was travelling with a WEC missionary, Mr. Coleman. We were stopped on the road by a Belgian Government official. He informed us that the ferry on the large Congo river, which we had to cross on our journey, had sunk. The ferry was constructed by a number of canoes fastened together, side by side. The official explained that the ferry men had neglected to bale out the water from the canoes, and when a large, loaded lorry drove onto the ferry, both it and the lorry sank. He said that it would be some days before the ferry could be raised as a team of local African divers had to be organized to unload the lorry. These divers do not use any breathing equipment so they have to make frequent trips to the surface for air. The official suggested that we book in at a government resthouse along the way, and spend a few days there until the ferry would be raised.

We took his advice and settled into the resthouse expecting to be delayed for a number of days. But when we woke up the first morning I was surprised to hear my fellow-traveller exclaim, 'We will be able to cross today!' He then told me that the Lord had given him a wonderful verse in his daily Bible reading that morning. He read it to me, 'Thus saith the Lord, which maketh a way in the sea, and a path in the mighty waters' (Isaiah 43:16).

We decided, in faith, to proceed to the river, and he was correct! When we arrived, we found a long queue of lorries which had been held up since the ferry sunk. We thought that even if the ferry had been raised, it would be a long, long time before all the lorries ahead of us could cross as only one lorry was allowed on the ferry each trip. But just as we parked in a position where we could not see the river because of the queue ahead of us, a roads' official approached us and told us to drive past the lorries to the river.

He said that the ferry had been floated, but was just making one more crossing before the ferrymen would be arrested on the opposite bank because of their careless neglect in failing to keep water baled out of the canoes. It was decided only to take small vehicles on the crossing and that was why we could pass the queue. My friend's faith was wonderfully rewarded, and we praised the Lord.

My time in Zaire came to an end. Isabel was on her way to Mombasa and I had a journey of hundreds of miles back across Uganda and Kenya to the east coast.

7

Our First Year Together in Africa

Isabel's arrival

I arrived in Mombasa a few days before Isabel was due, so I had the opportunity to find a suitable place to camp on the coast just a few miles south of the port. I say it was suitable, but the one difficulty that faced me was the fact that it was on a gravel site which would make it hard to pitch our small tent as the pegs for the ropes would not have much grip. And I could not erect the little tent until after Isabel's arrival as it would not have been safe to leave it unattended when I went to meet her.

The big day dawned and I was down at the docks very early, my eyes scanning the Indian Ocean for the first glimpse of the ship with its precious 'cargo'. Eventually on the horizon I saw the vague shape of a ship approaching. What thrill of excitement I experienced!

It took a little time before I could make out the figures of passengers lined along the deck rail, and I tried very hard as the ship drew nearer to pick out the liner's most important passenger, as far as I was concerned!

Then among the crowd, I saw her! I am not sure if my heart missed a beat as we waved vigorously to each other, but it was a moment of great excitement which increased as the time elapsed until she disembarked and I could have her in my arms.

Before starting off on our missionary travels together, we decided to have a two-week holiday beside the Indian Ocean in our 'new home' – the van and a tent. As I have mentioned, the gravel site made it difficult for the pegs to anchor the tent, so I fastened one or two of the guy ropes to the van. That resulted in a frightening incident just a few days after Isabel's arrival!

She was in the tent cooking some food on a primus stove and I was sitting out in the van reading when we had a very heavy rain storm. As I sat in the van, I saw a couple coming along the path nearby, getting thoroughly soaked with the rain. I took pity on them, and suggested that I give them a lift. They got into the vehicle and I began to drive away when, in my rear-view mirror, I noticed that I had pulled the tent down on top of Isabel! I had forgotten that the tent was fastened to the van. Fortunately, when I got out and rushed back, I found that although the tent had knocked Isabel, the primus and the food to the ground, the fall had extinguished the stove and avoided a fire before Isabel could creep out from under the canvas.

When I managed to help her out she was badly shaken and shocked, but soon we saw the funny side of what could have been a very bad accident. We thanked the Lord for his protection in spite of my carelessness. However, she admitted to me afterwards that she had wondered what kind of a man she had married. But there was more to come before our extended 'honeymoon' camp was over.

A Lion Chooses Its Supper

The tropical heat was quite intense so we usually slept in the tent with the door-flap wide open during the night. One morning a man informed us that during the night a lion had passed quite close, but ignoring our tent and its contents, went to a nearby village. It went over an eight foot fence and killed six goats! The next night we closed the flap of the tent, not that it would have done much good if the lion had decided to visit us. Again we were thankful that the Lord had looked after us.

When the two weeks of camping and getting to know each other a little better were over, we packed and prepared to start our journey which was to take us through part of Kenya, Tanganyika (now Tanzania), Northern Rhodesia (now Zambia),

Nyasaland (now Malawi), Southern Rhodesia (now Zimbabwe), Swaziland and South Africa.

When the tent had been packed away and tied on to the luggage rack, Isabel found that the van in which we were to travel was very cramped, to say the least. Quite a part of the space was taken up by cupboards and bunks, so the space in which we could move was very limited.

Isabel wrote about it later, 'Often in our travels, I would remember a poem I was taught at school: "I wish I lived in a caravan with a horse to drive like a peddler man."

'As a child I thought such a life would be wonderful. Well there I was, living in a van in which I could not stand up straight. To dress and undress I had to lie down on the bunk as the space and height were so limited. It was just as well that we did not have much in the way of material goods. Our cupboard space was very limited so we could only carry the bare necessities. The van had been fitted with a tiny handbasin, and I was just able to put my hands into it!

'We had what was called an "oso-cool". It was a little cupboard made of an absorbent material. It had a cavity on top to hold about half a pint of water, and the theory was that the water would soak into the material and as it evaporated it would keep the contents cool. However, in the tropical heat the theory did not work very well.

'The tent we had in those days was not like the modern type with windows, groundsheets etc., but at least I could stand in it. Then we had a tilley lamp and a small canvas bath. We had fun with both. When we hung the lamp in the tent at night, as well as giving off heat, it attracted hordes of flying tropical insects, so we had to close the tent door to keep them out! We discovered that it was better to hang the lamp on a tree outside with the door open – the light shone into the tent and the insects had their get-together outside. The tent was very much cooler that way.

'Our folding canvas bath – four feet square by eight inches deep – was held open by a small folding frame, it was so shallow that we could only use a small amount of water. Even then the water often splashed over, or the bath collapsed and emptied the contents. Water was not always available close by, often it had to be carried a distance. So living and travelling in the van was not all fun and games.'

What Isabel has said is a vivid picture of her life and travels with me in the van. I think I am safe in saying that very few women would have been willing for such a life with all its inconveniences, difficulties, dangers and loneliness. I have always been so thankful that the Lord gave me such a helpmeet and better half! I know that I could never have carried on without her help, fellowship, advice and counsel.

We started off south on our travels in September 1953. First, we called on some missionaries in the southern part of Kenya who had invited us. We could not inform them of the exact date of our visit as the condition of the clay roads determined how far we travelled each day.

Tanzania

We then crossed the border into Tanzania where we had the privilege of visiting mission stations and churches of the Church Missionary Society (Australian Section), The Swedish Free Mission, and the Moravian Mission. These visits resulted in many invitations to return at a later date, when arrangements would be made for special services.

On a Moravian Mission station, I had a welcome surprise to find that one of the missionary ministers on the station, the Rev. Dick Connor, had lived about two miles from my home when we were boys. His father was Bishop Connor in a Moravian village called Gracehill, but his son Dick had gone to boarding school in England. So we had never met in Ireland as my family belonged to the Presbyterian church and attended local schools. We met for the first time many thousands of miles from our boyhood haunts!

When Dick knew that I had come to represent a Missionary Training School, he took me on a ten hour walk into the mountains to see an unmanned mission station. He wanted to impress on me the shortage of Moravian missionaries and hoped that I might be able to do some recruiting. Isabel remained with his wife Sheila at their mission house, while Dick and I spent a few days on the empty station. We had to stay a little longer than we had planned as I sprained my knee climbing up the mountain path to the mission.

It was a beautiful mission station in the mountains and had been built by German missionaries before the second world war. As Tanzania was part of British East Africa, the German missionaries were required by the British Authorities to make a declaration that they opposed Hitler's aggression. Those who refused to do so had to leave the country, hence the shortage of missionaries. I was able later to locate an American missionary and his wife who were willing to fill the vacancy, but before the arrangements could be made for them to travel, the Moravian Mission had found suitable staff.

I had the privilege before leaving Tanzania of being asked by a missionary to go to his house and have special prayer with him. I found him very depressed and discouraged because he was not seeing spiritual fruit from his ministry. He then told me that he was packing his bags to go home because he did not have real victory over sin in his own life and so he felt he could not remain and preach to the Africans. He went on to describe how he had given up and gone home once before. When he got there he was so convicted because he had run away from the work that God had given him to do that he repented and returned. Then the same situation had arisen again.

I spent some time in counselling him and we looked at verses like Romans 6:14: 'Sin shall not have dominion over you.' The conditions for such victorious Christian living depended on full surrender to the Holy Spirit and full obedience to His revealed will.

When we knelt in prayer the missionary had difficulty in praying. It was evident that there was something on his mind. Something stood between him and full surrender to the Lord. Then he suddenly said, 'Lord, You know that thing you always wanted me to do and I have not been willing to do it. I am now willing to do it.' As soon as he made that promise to the Lord, he rose from his knees with the joy of the Lord radiating from his face. He told me that when God had asked him to go to Africa, He impressed on him that he should sell his business and give the money to missionary work. But he had put some of the money aside for himself in case things did not work out in Africa! That had left him an escape route to go back to business if things became difficult. But there was not complete trust in the Lord and disobedience was hindering his faith.

After that commitment to the Lord, he did not go home! Instead he opened up a new mission work in an area where no missionaries worked, and he spent around thirty more years there successfully working for the Lord before he reached retirement age. At the time of writing his son is in charge of the work he started.

Malawi

From Tanzania, we crossed into Malawi. Our first stop was in the village of one of Malawi's senior chiefs, Chief Mtwalo. What a surprise we got when we heard him speak English. He spoke like a Highlander! Then we discovered that he had been taught English in the mission schools by missionaries from Scotland. He gave us a great welcome and provided sleeping accommodation for us. It was not long before I was involved in repairing a watch at the request of a villager.

A sad event took place at our next stop. We were camping near a river during the time of the year when there are heavy rain storms, and it was because of flooding that the sad incident occurred. The river had so swollen that it washed away the only bridge in the area. As a result, people began to gather on each bank, waiting for the level of the water in the river to go down so that they could wade across. Among those waiting was a messenger from the Education Department who was carrying wages for teachers.

He did not want to sit around on the bank as he was afraid the money might be stolen, so as soon as he thought the river level was low enough he tried to cross to the other bank. When he was part of the way, he noticed that a large wall of water was approaching from a heavy downfall in the mountains upstream. There was no time to reach either bank, so he quickly climbed a tree that was growing near him in the flooded area and sat on one of the branches.

Suddenly he saw an angry, poisonous snake being swept downstream in the current. He got quite a shock when the snake decided to do what he had done – it began to climb the tree! He had to decide which of the two he would face, the roaring current of the river or the angry snake. He decided that the snake was worse than the water, so he jumped off the tree into the river. But it was only a matter of seconds before the raging torrent bashed him against rocks and he died. I have sometimes used that incident in sermons to illustrate the awful power of the current of addiction to sinful habits. No-one could save that young man as the current was too strong. But with the current of sin, there is One who can save and rescue the sinner – Jesus.

Another event resulted in much joy for us. A young man stopped at our camp out of curiosity to know who we were, and when he discovered we were missionaries he said that there was a missionary doctor and his family a few miles from where we were camping. He explained how to reach his station. We found out from the young man that he was referring to was a son of Dr. Clive Irvine of Chogoria in Kenya. I have mentioned Clive in an earlier chapter. Clive had given us his son Ken's address, but we did not realise that our camping place was so close to his mission hospital. Being in Malawi for the first time, the address did not mean much to us as we had not yet obtained a map.

We did not waste much time before going to see Ken and his family. Little did we know that it was to be the beginning of a long-lasting, close fellowship and friendship with the family and that it would, some months later, result in opening up many years of service for us in Malawi.[1]

Our next main contact in Malawi was with the missionaries of the South African Dutch Reformed Church Mission. Their early missionaries in 1880s went to Malawi under the influence of the late Andrew Murray, the well-known author of many devotional books. He arranged, being a Scot himself, with Dr. Laws of Livingstonia to send missionaries to help with the work in Malawi. By 1889 the Presbyterian church in Malawi had three 'mother' churches providing missionaries – The United Free Church in the north, the Dutch Reformed Church in the centre, and the Church of Scotland in the south. In 1926 the churches which had been planted in all three regions united as The Church of Central Africa Presbyterian.

Isabel became ill and a South African mission doctor diagnosed appendicitis. The doctor arranged for me to take her over one hundred miles to the government hospital in Zomba, which

---

1. Although it is getting ahead of events, the reader should know that during the years we spent in Malawi, Ken and I worked together in evangelism and the preparation of literature for young converts, until the Lord called him to higher service in 1978. His wife Elsabe and Isabel were very close friends in Malawi, and Elsabe was a great companion to Isabel especially when I was away on preaching appointments. They are still in quite close touch as Elsabe has retired in Edinburgh.

was the capital of the country at that time. As I have mentioned, it was the season of the rains and the roads were very muddy. On our way to the hospital we found five vehicles stuck in the mud and I had to help to extract them, so our journey took longer than we expected. Eventually we arrived at the home of the Rev. Andrew and Barbara Doig, as Andrew was the Church of Scotland missionary in Zomba at that time and the doctor had informed him that we were on our way.

Andrew made the arrangements for Isabel to be admitted to the hospital, and I was given accommodation in their home during the period of her stay for the operation. We cannot forget their kindness to us in such an emergency.[2]

During the time Isabel was in hospital I came close to having a very serious and probably fatal accident. I had jacked-up the van to change the tyres around and do some repairs underneath. I had been lying under the van working and came out to do or get something, when suddenly the supports collapsed and the van dropped to the ground as I had removed the wheels. Had I still been underneath I do not see how I could have escaped death. With a thankful heart to the Lord, I promised never again to use that method of raising a vehicle! (Although I am a 'Jack'.)

After the operation was over, the surgeon kept Isabel in hospital for an extended time as he was afraid we would start travelling too soon, seeing we did not have a home of our own in which to rest. When she did get out, Andrew and Barbara would not allow us to leave until we had a few days holiday, so they arranged for us to use the Mission Cottage on the top of Zomba mountain – a famous spot in Malawi for holidays. We enjoyed our time there very much, apart from one evening when there was a very strong earth tremor and the cottage, being near the edge of the mountain, felt rather insecure!

When Isabel was strong enough to travel, the time had come

2. Andrew later became a Moderator of the Church of Scotland.

for us to leave Malawi. Our passage had been booked on a ship from Cape Town, and although there were about nine months left, we had over 2,000 miles to travel and quite a number of calls to make.

On our way out of Malawi we camped one night by a school. The African headmaster came to greet us and I had the opportunity for a long talk with him. During our conversation I asked him how long he had been a Christian. He answered, 'I was born a Christian.' When I asked him to explain how that happened, he said that both his parents were Christians.

I then explained to him that I too had Christian parents, but that did not stop me doing some sinful things as I was growing up. I told him that it was when I reached the age of thirteen that I was convicted of my sin and realised the need to be forgiven and changed by Jesus so that I could live a Christian life.

He then said, 'Jesus has sent you here tonight. I have been planning to send away my wife and take another girl. Will you pray for me so that I can be forgiven for my sins and be a real Christian?' I had the joy of pointing him to the Saviour. I was very glad to meet him in later years and to find out that he had become a minister in a church of the Zambesi Mission.

Zambia

From Malawi we crossed into Zambia, but on the way we had a serious wheelbearing problem. The garage across the border in a government centre in Zambia called Fort Jameson informed us that bearings for our van were not available locally. The little Bedford Dormobile we had, was one of the first to be produced, and spares had not arrived in such an isolated spot as Fort Jameson in Zambia. We were told that it would take some time for the garage to obtain them from South Africa or Zimbabwe. Transport of goods was not very fast in that part of the world so we were 'marooned' in the centre of Africa!.

However, the Good Shepherd does not lose sight of His

sheep. He knew all about our problem and had a solution ready. We remembered that when we visited Ken and Elsabe Irvine in Malawi, they mentioned that if ever we were passing through Fort Jameson in Zambia, there was a Christian sanitary inspector and his family living there – Jack and Ruth Holmes. I asked the Immigration Officer who was stamping our passports if the Holmes still lived in the centre. He said they were still there and if we would follow his car he would lead us to their house! Which he did.

We knocked at the door and Ruth answered. When we tried to introduce ourselves and explain that we had a problem, she told us that she was expecting us! Elsabe Irvine had sent on socks I had left behind when we stayed there and she informed the Holmes that we might call! We received a very warm and enthusiastic welcome, with the invitation to stay with them until the parts for the van arrived. The Lord had gone ahead and made arrangements for us.

That was the beginning of a lasting friendship with the family during the years we were in Africa. Many times we had the privilege and joy of staying in their home when we were passing on future trips in both Malawi and Zambia (Jack moved around in the government service). Those visits meant much to us as a welcome break from the confinement of the van, and the spiritual fellowship was refreshing.

It was so relaxing to spend time playing with their children too on some of those occasions. Although one night I gave them a great fright. In the dark, I hid behind a large rock in the garden, and when the children came out I imitated the roar of a lion. What a rush there was back into the house, for I also gave the parents a fright! But a number of years later, I had the privilege of counselling their oldest daughter, Margaret, when she wanted to invite the Lord Jesus into her life. The friendship with the family is still continuing, although both of us have retired to Britain. So the van's problems were allowed by the

Lord for a purpose, reminding us that 'all things work together for good' when the Shepherd is leading His flock.

Jack Holmes told us of an interesting but damaging incident that they had experienced. Jack was due a holiday and arranged for the family to go away. He left a young man to look after his house, garden and chickens until they returned. During his holiday, because of some emergency in the health department, Jack was called back to his office. After attending to the problem he called at his house to see how the young man was managing. What a shocking surprise he had!

The young man had decided to brew a large drum of maize beer and had invited his friends to come to the house for a party. He wore his master's suit to entertain them! They used the carpeted lounge for their celebrations, and when some could not go home because of the hangover, they were given beds. The house was in an awful state. What an illustration, which I have used many times, of Jesus' parable about the servant whose master 'will come on a day when he does not expect him' (Matthew 24:50).

But to get back to 1954 and our stay in Fort Jameson with the family. We were introduced to a young missionary couple while we were with the Holmes – James and Betty Veitch. James was the manager of a leprosarium some miles from the government centre under the Dutch Reformed Mission. The Veitchs and the Holmes had very good Christian fellowship together. The reason I mention James and Betty here is because a very sad event followed shortly afterwards, showing sacrifices that missionaries make.

Betty was pregnant, but later she had some complications and it was decided to fly her to Pretoria in South Africa so that she could have the baby delivered where there were specialist facilities. After her arrival and before the baby was born, she took very ill and in spite of the medical efforts made to treat her, she went into a coma and died. It was later discovered that the consultant dealing with her case had not been told that she had been brought down from the tropics, so he had not suspected cerebral malaria which had caused her death. It was a very trying time for James.

The Lord is no man's debtor

After the van was repaired we left Zambia, drove through Zimbabwe and arrived in Johannesburg, South Africa where an invitation was waiting for us to visit a mission station of the Africa Evangelical Fellowship in Swaziland. We had a very interesting experience there in which the Lord taught us a wonderful lesson.

While we were on the station we received a request to have breakfast with an independent missionary couple who lived nearby. After we came away from their home, both Isabel and I felt that the Lord wanted us to give them a gift of some money although the good breakfast we had enjoyed did not give us the impression that they were in need. Also we knew that we just had enough money for petrol and expenses to cover the remaining 1,300 miles to the boat in Cape Town! However, the impression remained with both of us that it was the Lord's guidance that we should give, so we sent the money to their house.

Three very interesting things happened on our way south. We had to travel back through Johannesburg, where we had been asked to visit a man who provided missionaries with equipment such as radio telephones. When we were saying goodbye to him, he slipped something into my hand – it turned out to be the exact amount of money we had sent to the missionaries in Swaziland that morning!

We had also given an address in Johannesburg to friends in case anyone wanted to contact us on our trip south. When we called to see if any correspondence had arrived, we found a letter with a cheque for a substantial amount, with the instruction that it was to help us on our way!

The third item which made us marvel at the Lord's guidance when He asked us to give up money that we felt we needed, was only revealed to us later when we reached Cape Town. There was a letter from the missionaries we had helped, informing us that when they invited us for the meal, they went out to a shop and spent the last of their money to provide for us. They had no money left for their next meal when our money arrived. In the letter they not only thanked us, but they were praising the Lord for His provision.

In Cape Town we had the privilege of visiting some of the areas where I had worked from 1948 to 1951. The congregation which I had the privilege of helping to plant had already grown to two in the three years since I had left, and it continued to grow.

We also had the opportunity for fellowship with a number of the missionaries with whom I worked during those years and to hear details of how the Lord was blessing. Time was limited, however, as our sailing date only gave us a couple of weeks there, and we boarded the ship for the fifteen-day sailing to Southampton.

8

Invitations to Return

As a result of our first trip to Central and Southern Africa, Isabel and I received many invitations to return to mission areas for special meetings – to speak at conferences, seminars, gatherings of students, etc. As a result of these invitations we had to make a number of decisions when we were back in Britain:

1. Was it the Lord's will for us to continue with our trips in Africa?
2. If so, how should the next tour be organised? Where would it start and finish? Which invitations should we accept?
3. How long should it last?
4. How would it be financed?

In praying over whether it was the Lord's will for us to go back to Africa, Isabel had a secret spiritual struggle which she did not reveal to me right away as she knew that I loved Africa and wanted to go back. I will let her describe it herself:

'I must confess that I did not find it easy to live and travel in the cramped quarters of the van, especially with the African roads and tropical conditions. I could remember the dust pouring into the van through the windows which had to be kept open because of the heat, and the times we stuck in the mud and in a river all night. I found it very difficult to face another tour, so I told the Lord that I just could not go back to Africa again. Jack was not aware of that as I had not told him, but at a Christian conference we were attending, the

Lord dealt with me in such a way that finally I yielded and said to the Lord, "Even if it means going back to live in that little van again, I am willing."

'Within ten days of making that promise, we were given a larger van to take with us the next time (we had brought the other smaller van back to Britain). I could stand upright in the new van! God was just waiting for my willingness. I am glad that I made the right choice and surrendered to His will.'

That was the spiritual battle that Isabel had fought and won with the Lord's help. I am so glad she did win, because if she had continued to feel that there was too much self-sacrifice in returning to Africa we would have had to settle down to some other type of work with the guilty feeling that we had deviated from what the Lord wanted with our lives and service.

When we both were convinced that it was the Lord's will for us to go back to Africa, we had to face the question of finance. Our first trip was sponsored by the Mission School in Glasgow, under its evangelism branch Message of Victory Evangelism known as MOVE. It was a factfinding experience for that department, as well as seeking to minister where opportunities arose. But on the second trip we would have to take the final responsibility for the expenses. MOVE was a home mission department and the trustees did not feel that they could commit themselves to take full responsibility for overseas work.

However, Isabel and I were so convinced that because the Lord wanted us to go back to Africa He would provide for us if we took the step of faith. The trustees would send on any donations received for the tour, and agreed to give us a letter stating that they would arrange for us to get home in the event of any serious problem.

We decided that we would never ask anyone for money. We would bring our needs to the Lord in prayer and trust Him to provide. In a wonderful way enough money was provided for our fare back to Africa and to get us started on our second tour of the continent. Among the invitations we received were some to Malawi, Tanzania and Kenya. We felt the best way to accept these would be in that order. We would sail back to Cape Town and travel north from there, first of all to Loudon mission station in Malawi where the Rev. Vernon Stone, a Church of Scotland missionary and the local African minister invited us to conduct a four week evangelistic mission in their area in January 1956.

We sailed in the autumn of 1955. Our new van had been shipped earlier and was waiting for us in Cape Town. I left Isabel to clear our personal luggage with the Custom's Officer while I went to arrange to clear the van and its contents. When I arrived back at the passenger terminal, Isabel saw me and shouted for me to come, but to my surprise the officer also called, 'Jack, come here!'

When I reached them, Isabel explained that he wanted the model number of a record player which was at the bottom of a large wooden box. (Actually it was only the bare mechanism of the player and was to be used to play records over an amplifier in open-air meetings; we had bought it for a few shillings in the 'barrows' in Glasgow.) Isabel had tried to explain to him that we were not leaving it in South Africa but were taking it out with us when we went north. Yet he demanded that she open the box so that he could see it. He had been quite angry with the passenger who was ahead of her as it seems she tried to deceive him, so his mood was not too friendly.

The lid of the box was screwed down, but Isabel had a screwdriver in her bag in case we had to open it, which she handed to him and asked him to open it! Not the best way to make friends with a Custom's officer! But apparently he saw the funny side of it as he tried to find the player among other equipment in the large box – hence the call for me to come and locate it which I did. When he had seen it and we had closed the box and were about to leave, he looked at Isabel, and with a big smile said, 'Half an hour with you has done me good!'

Revival in Malawi

We had interesting times of visits and fellowship with missionaries, church workers and other Christians on our way to Malawi. It was December 1955 when we approached the border. As a couple of missionaries on Loudon mission station, Eric Jeffery and Carol Wilson, were to be married during the first week of January, we felt it best to postpone our arrival until after the wedding, as our special services were to commence in the second week of the month.

We decided to park our van in an isolated spot before we reached the border, so that we could have concentrated prayer for the meetings which were to be held. We knew that without the Holy Spirit nothing would be accomplished for eternity. We prayed that the Lord would help us to be like the good spies who searched for and brought back excellent 'fruit' to show the Israelites what God had prepared for them. We wanted the Holy Spirit to help us to witness to the wonderful spiritual 'fruit' He has in store for all who will follow Him into the 'land' of His full salvation.

Unknown to us at the time, Vernon had arranged a ministers' retreat for all the Presbyterian ministers in the north of Malawi. It was to take place during the first week of the evangelistic services. I was to speak to the ministers in the morning and in the other meetings in the afternoon.

When we arrived on the station and we were informed of the programme, I had to quickly prepare the studies for the ministers. I felt drawn to take the subject of 'Sanctification' which resulted in helpful discussions. The ministers also attended the afternoon services. As a result of attending the retreat and the evangelistic services, the ministers felt that it was not right for only one congregation to have special meetings.

Because of their pleading and keenness for services, we changed our plans and agreed to visit most of their congregations, as will be seen by the following reports of reviving in their churches. Instead of spending four weeks as originally planned, Isabel and I spent eight months in the north of the country and even then we were not able to visit all the areas which would have liked special services.

When the evangelistic services commenced in Loudon church, a missionary on the station asked me, 'Have you ever seen an African really convicted of sin? I have been here for twelve and a half years, and I have not. Yes, when you find out that something wrong had been done, and you challenge a person, he will often say he is sorry, but one feels it is just because the fault has been discovered.' I explained that we had seen genuine conviction and repentance resulting in transformed lives.

At first the spiritual atmosphere of the services in the afternoon was most discouraging. Isabel and I were very concerned as we could not sense the awareness of the Holy Spirit, so we decided not to eat or sleep until we had the assurance that the Lord would overcome the hindrances. We did not know until later that my interpreter, the minister of the congregation, was secretly involved in adultery.

After waiting on the Lord for some time, we saw a spirit of conviction for sin coming into the services and a number of people came for counselling. Two of those who were converted during that first month of meetings, one a teacher and the other a student, entered the ministry of the church later.

A transformed school

When the services at Loudon were over, we moved to our next invitation about 30 miles north to what was called a Government Boma, that is, a centre of local government, with a hospital, police station, a magistrate and a court room. The centre of the congregation to which we were invited was close to a large boarding school.

We arrived in the village on a Monday afternoon and the services started on Tuesday. On Wednesday morning, a sixteen-year-old boy called Kenneth came to our van saying that he had not slept all night because the words he had heard the day before had caused him to remember his sins during the night. He had come for prayer so that his sins could be forgiven. We had the joy of pointing him to the Saviour for forgiveness and cleansing. Later in the day he came back asking if he could wash dishes for us or do some other work as a way of thanking us for telling him about Jesus! On Thursday he brought another student and said, 'I have been telling this boy about Jesus and he wants to be His follower too.'

That reminded us of the Samaritan woman who when she found Jesus and the Living Water went to the village and said, 'Come see a man who has told me all the things I have ever done: is not this the Christ?' And that afternoon, as a new convert, she brought more people to Jesus than many Christians have done all their lives.

Some days later I met the local magistrate, and he said to me, 'Something unusual has happened. A boy came to me and admitted that he had been in my garden and had stolen some carrots. He then asked me to forgive him.' The magistrate thought that it was a remarkable change for a boy to come and admit he had done wrong. It was our friend Kenneth who, although he knew that Jesus had forgiven him, wanted also to be forgiven by the one from whom he had stolen.

From that time, other boarders approached us in groups, under deep conviction for sin, admitting thefts of chickens, fruit, vegetables and even a cow! When closing up the tent one night, we saw a little oil lamp approaching with a number of black legs behind it. It was a group of the boarders who could not sleep because of conviction for their sins. They had risen from their beds so that they could come to pray for forgiveness. They had seen the joy in the lives of the others who had accepted Jesus as their Saviour.

Eventually we were told that every boy in the dormitory – only boys boarded – had come for prayer and counselling, except one. He was very opposed to the idea of admitting that he was a sinner. He was a member of a sect which allowed sinful practices among its members, such as polygamy and drunkenness.

However, before the week of meetings had ended, the boarders awoke early one morning because the unrepentant boy was sobbing loudly. When they gathered around his bed, he said, 'I have had a dream in which I have seen Jesus. He stood by my bed and said to me, "Why are you closing the door of your heart to Me and opening it for Satan?"' All in the dormitory then joined with him in prayer until 5.00 am when they called the headmaster, who joined with them in prayer until 6.00. Then they all came to the tent where the lad trusted Christ to forgive him and promised to follow Him.

But I must tell you about the headmaster. I will call him Edward, although that is not his proper name. He was a church member and he asked me if Isabel and I would come to his house to pray for him and his wife. When we arrived in his home, he told us that he was doing further studies by correspondence and tried to use as much time as possible in his lunch hour to work on his lectures. But quite often when he arrived at his house for lunch, he would find that his wife was out talking to the neighbouring women and had not started to prepare his food. That made him very angry. Now he was convicted for how he treated his wife on such occasions. He wanted prayer so that he could overcome his temper.

I said, 'Edward, you need more than prayer, you need to be "born again" as Jesus told Nicodemus.'

Like Nicodemus, he asked how that could take place and we had the joy of sharing with him the portions of Scripture which point out the way of salvation, including how Jesus gives us a spiritual rebirth through the Holy Spirit coming to dwell within us. We showed him that it was not our bodies that needed to be reborn, but the spirit within us which controls our bodies and our minds. We considered what Jesus said: 'That which is born of the flesh is flesh; and that which is born of the Spirit is spirit' (John 3:6). We explained to him that the Holy Spirit implants the mind of Christ within us when we are born again.

We then suggested that he find a quiet place where he could be alone with the Lord and ask the Holy Spirit to make the way of salvation clear to him through His Word which we had shared together. Later he told us that he had followed our suggestion and had invited Jesus into his life. He had the assurance that his sins were forgiven and that he was a new person in Christ.

He said, 'As I prayed and went over Scripture, a light brighter than the sun shone around me, when the assurance of acceptance with God came. My joy was so great that I did not sleep for two nights. On the second night I saw two mountains, although I was not asleep. On one mountain there were people doing many sinful things and on the other there were people dressed in white, praising and worshipping God. I felt that God was saying to me, "Your work in life is to lead people from the mountain of sin to the mountain of holiness." I feel that God is calling me to the ministry and I have promised to obey Him.'

Soon after his conversion, a Government Educational Officer who was a white man came to him and said, 'Edward, I want to congratulate you as your school has come out third in the whole country for passes this year. The Education Department has decided to send you to a university in England for a degree course, and you will come back to be an Education Officer.'

He refused the offer saying, 'God has called me to be a min-

ister in the church and I cannot accept the department's offer.'
Of course, it was a big temptation for Edward as degrees were
greatly coveted in the country which did not have its own university at the time, and he would have had a greatly increased
salary on his return.

The officer told him, 'You are a fool to refuse this offer.
You will never have an opportunity like this again!' But he
kept his promise to the Lord and entered theological training,
dropping from his headmaster's salary to a very small Church
allowance while he was in training. He also knew that when he
would be ordained, his stipend would be much lower than the
salary he had as a headmaster. After a few years of ministry, he
was granted a church bursary to study for a Bachelor of Divinity degree with London University through the London Bible
College.

But to get back to our week of meetings in Mzimba: there
were many others as well as students who came for counselling. Some days during that week, Isabel and I spent up to ten
hours counselling men, women and children who came to the
tent for prayer. Eventually we found it too difficult to get the
necessary time for the effective counselling of each individual,
so we sent back to Loudon and asked the missionary who had
said he had never seen a person really convicted during all the
years he had worked in Africa if he could come and help us.
When he arrived, he spent four hours in the tent with a group of
young men seeking forgiveness for sins they had covered up in
their lives. When he emerged from the tent, he shook himself,
and said, 'I have never had such an experience in all my years
of missionary work.'

Many lives were transformed during those days and there
were some remarkable conversions. Let me share one or two of
them with you:

A detective is 'arrested'

Thomas, which is not his proper name, was a detective who attended the evangelistic services. He was convicted by the Word of the Lord for the way he had been living, although he was a member of the church. He came for prayer and told us how his detective work took him away from home. During his official investigations he spent a lot of time with prostitutes under the guise of doing detective work. He had tried to reform his life, but found it too difficult to give up his immoral ways. When it was pointed out to him that he could become a 'new person' in Christ through the new birth, he looked at me in amazement. We knelt on the ground beside the tent as I tried to explain to him simply the way of repentance, forgiveness, faith and commitment of himself to Christ who had died for him. Thomas prayed, asking for forgiveness, expressing sorrow for his sinful life and inviting Jesus to come into his life and change him so that he could live a true Christian life.

When he rose from his knees he looked very solemn, but mounting his bicycle, he said he would be back later. When he returned after some time his face was radiant, and with joy he told us, 'I went home and talked to my wife, explaining to her the way I had been living in the villages when I was away on duty. She has forgiven me, and Jesus has forgiven me, and now I am very happy,' and he certainly showed it. Some weeks later when I saw him, he told me that when temptations came to him, he found that he had no desire for the old life!

An immigration officer admits a new 'immigrant'

An immigration officer who attended the services came to the tent in a very agitated state. It was evident that he was under deep conviction for his sins. He said that his job was to issue entry permits at the border to immigrants wishing to enter Malawi. Sometimes when a woman came to his office to apply for a permit, he promised to give it if she would agree to have sex with him. Under the Word of God he had been convicted and was sorry for his sin. A new Person was now applying for permission to enter, not the country, but into his heart and life. He heard the knock at the 'office door' of his heart, and heard Someone saying, 'If any man hear my voice, and open the door, I will come in to him' (Revelation 3:20). In prayer he repented of his immoral conduct, and after being shown the way of salvation he invited the 'Heavenly Immigrant' to enter his heart and life.

Space does not allow me to linger longer reporting the work of the Holy Spirit's reviving in that village, except to mention that it was one of the most outstanding weeks in all our years of ministry. Isabel and I felt so near to the Lord and the things of 'earth grew strangely dim, in the light of His Glory and grace!' as we saw boys and girls, men and women realise the sinfulness of sin when they came face to face with a holy God. Then to see the evidence of the grace and mercy of God in the joy of forgiveness in their transformed lives.

But it was only when the meetings came to an end that we realised how exhausted we were physically, emotionally and mentally. Before getting involved in the weeks of meetings ahead, we felt it would be good to get away for a few days to a spot where no-one knew us so that we could 'recharge our spiritual batteries' and also renew our physical energy.

Malawi has a lovely lake, now called Lake Malawi, but previously known as Lake Nyasa. It is around 380 miles long and has an average width of over 50 miles. Our services were held about 60 miles from the lake, so we decided it would be nice to spend a few days there as it would be our first visit.

The morning after we arrived some men were standing near the van. When we greeted them, they asked, 'When are you going to preach to us?' News of the meetings 60 miles away had reached them. The 'bush telegraph' was operating. I must admit that when I saw the hope of our few days of rest when I would not have to preach for a few days fading, the words of Ahab to Elijah flashed into my mind, 'Hast thou found me, O mine enemy?' (1 Kings 21:20). I felt convicted afterwards as I thought how welcome that request would be in Moslem lands!

Extension of campaign

We had only been invited to Malawi for one month of special services. But ministers of other congregations of the Presbyterian Church begged us to extend our stay and hold services in their areas and so we spent eight months there instead of the one.

It would make this account much too long to report in detail the events of each series of services during that period. I will only share some of the ways in which we saw the Lord reviving His church and changing lives.

Accounts are Rectified

After a service in a village, a civil servant who was interpreting my talk to the congregation came and asked if he could speak to me. (We will call him Fred). He told me the following:

'While I was interpreting the Word of God for you, words have stuck in my heart. I am an accountant in a government office and some time ago I took £17.50 out of the safe and managed to 'doctor' the books so it has never been discovered. How may I receive forgiveness from God?'

'First of all,' I explained, 'you must be sorry before God for sinning. Only by coming to Jesus can your sins be forgiven, because He took our punishment for us when He died on the cross. But like Zacchaeus, if you are really repenting and truly sorry for your sins, you will go to your supervisor and explain what has happened and promise to refund the money as soon as you can. That won't merit forgiveness but it will show how sorry you are for what you have done and that you do not want to retain anything that does not rightfully belong to you.'

Fred looked at me anxiously, and said: 'I cannot do that. I am a civil servant, and I have committed a very serious crime in Government eyes. The punishment is imprisonment, dismissal and no pension.'

I told him, 'You have to decide which is more important, the fear of losing your job or receiving peace with God. If you promise to put the matter right, God will forgive you, just as Jesus said to Zacchaeus when he promised to give back the extra money he had taken from people when he collected their taxes, "Today, salvation has come to this house", even though he had not yet had any opportunity to see the people. Repaying the money will not buy forgiveness from God, but it is the sign of true repentance and sorrow for sin, as Paul explains in 2 Corinthians 7:9, 10. When you receive the joy of God's forgiveness, Fred, and you know that you are born again, you will have the strength to go and put the matter right.'

After the meetings in that village, I did not see Fred again for about two years. But when I did see him he had an exciting story to tell. He had gone to the supervisor, a white man. He was treated very kindly and allowed to repay the money as he was able. No disciplinary action was taken against him. Shaking hands with him, the supervisor said, 'I am glad to meet an honest man.'

Fred was promoted later and sent overseas by the Government to take advanced training, and on his return he was appointed to a very important Government position which takes him to different parts of the world representing his country at important international conferences.

Would-be murderer throws away her poison

While I was talking to Fred, a woman approached Isabel and asked for prayer. We will call her Grace. She then told Isabel that she and her husband had been happily married and had lived together for many years. But she had been in hospital recently and when she came home she discovered that her husband had taken a second wife. (Under traditional law in Malawi that was permissible.)

Grace then went on to say that she had become so angry with her husband, she had gone to a witchdoctor to obtain poison and actually had the poison with her in her bag! She had intended to put the poison secretly into the food which the second wife would be cooking for her husband. She then told Isabel that the Word of God which she had just heard in the church had convicted her and she wanted to repent and seek forgiveness. She promised that she would destroy the poison. After counselling and prayer, she left Isabel saying that the great burden of jealousy and murder had gone.

It is interesting to note that a short time later her husband sent away the second wife, and once again Grace had a happy home life. When independence was granted to Malawi, her husband was given a high post in the diplomatic service. What a different situation would have developed if she had not given herself to Jesus and destroyed the poison.

Owner receives lost spectacles after thirty years

An elderly man, after listening intently to the preaching in a service, came to me with a pair of spectacles and said, 'I was the house-servant in the home of a missionary who lived here many years ago. One day when he was out of the house and left these spectacles on the table, I decided to take them for myself. When he came back he looked all over for them, but I denied having seen them. Now God has spoken to me and I want them to be sent back to him,' he said, as he handed them to me. He told me the name of the missionary, and I knew that he worked for a Glasgow evening paper.

On our next leave in Scotland I went to see the ex-missionary and handed him his spectacles, telling him the story his servant had told me. He was amazed, saying that it was thirty years since he had lost them! He wrote an interesting article in the newspaper about how spectacles, lost for thirty years, had been found!

Students for the Ministry

I have previously referred to four of the young men who were converted during that time of reviving in the church entered the ministry. Three are still very active in the Lord's work, having given over thirty years of faithful service to His Church.

The fourth minister, Richard Ndolo, died of cancer at the end of 1994. He was one of Malawi's best preachers, but did not always find it easy to be a true servant of the Lord. In one charge where the chief was a polygamist and local politicians were living immoral lives, he felt that it was his duty to speak out against these sinful things. As a result, the politicians asked the Presbytery to arrange for his removal from the charge.

Unfortunately, in a 'one-party' state where opposition to the political party could mean detention or even death without trial, the Presbytery succumbed. The minister was posted to a very isolated charge. While there his wife became very ill and died before medical aid could be obtained. That caused a great upheaval in the life of Richard as his children were young and still at school, but it did not deter him from accepting a large congregation later. He had a fruitful ministry as a widower. He told me that he never wanted to remarry as he and his wife had been joined together as one by the Lord and he could not consider having anyone else. When I was back in Malawi in 1994, I had the privilege of spending some time with him on two occasions. He was very ill at the time, but was still full of the joy of the Lord he loved to serve.

Preaching nonsense(?)

One of the ministers who invited us to hold services in his congregation had a problem. The missionary in his area was not an evangelical, but one who questioned and dismissed certain portions of Scripture. When he heard of the minister's invitation to me, he was upset and advised him to cancel the special services. The missionary did not have authority to stop him, and the minister who knew how other congregations had been revived decided not to take his advice.

During my first service, the missionary sat restlessly on the front seat, taking notes. I was preaching on the subject of the 'new birth' and it was evident that he was very uncomfortable with my talk.

When I left the church I went for a walk so that I could pray, as I was very troubled about the effect the missionary's attitude could have on the services. When I returned to the house where we were staying, Isabel said to me, 'The missionary has been here to see you, and he will be back at 8.00 pm.' Having a good idea of why he was coming I prayed for guidance.

When he arrived and before he sat down, he said, 'Jack, that was a lot of nonsense you preached today. If God would change us, as you described today, we would become so proud that God could not handle us. We must keep on sinning to keep us humble.'

I suddenly thought of the words of Spurgeon, 'You don't need to defend the Bible, it is like a lion. Let it out and it will fend for itself!' So when he sat down, I asked him to give me the meaning of verses in the Bible which emphasised the need to be 'born again', as well as verses which tell of the great change that such an experience brings into the life of a believer. We reached the Scripture which states, 'God is able to make all grace abound toward you; that ye, always having all sufficiency in all things, may abound to every good work' (2 Corinthians 9:8). He then jumped off his chair and said, 'I will have to go and consult my commentary on that one,' and he named a non-evangelical commentary!

However, if what I preached was 'nonsense', it appeared to reap a good harvest, as a teenage boy and a teenage girl sought counsel after the service and experienced the great change which Jesus promised. The boy, who later became a manager with a large international organization, has maintained a strong Christian witness during the forty years since he made that decision. He has been very active in his church, in the Scripture Union and other youth work.

The girl went on to become a secondary school teacher and taught in a large girls' school, taking a great spiritual interest in the welfare of the girls as well as their education. Unfortunately she became ill with tuberculosis, but she was allergic to the drugs given, and they resulted in an attack of hepatitis which was not diagnosed until she went into a coma and died. It was hard for us to understand why a young woman so promising in her profession, and especially in her love for the Lord and desire to see her students dedicate their lives to Christ, should have had such a short few years for service. We could only conclude that the Lord needed her for some special appointment in the heavenly homeland!

I had one other case of opposition to the evangelical message from a senior missionary when he would not allow the minister to arrange the meetings on the station where he was in charge.

Second Visit to Tanzania

As a result of our first trip, we had received other invitations for special services as well as the one from Malawi – two of these were to Tanzania and one to Kenya. After eight months in Malawi, we felt the time had come to go north. The Rev. Dick Connor had invited us back to have special services for secondary school students. There was a large school with many students and Dick was the principal.

When we arrived from Malawi, the meetings had been arranged and once again we had the privilege of ministering to young people who were starting out on the journey of life. We counted it a great privilege. Also having fellowship with the large number of missionaries on the station who came from different countries was an invaluable experience. The seven-year old son of one of the families with whom we were having a meal fascinated us. The mother and father were French speaking, so that was the language of the home. We were English speaking; the maid who worked in the home spoke Nyakyusa, a local language; and the African minister spoke Swahili. The little boy could speak to each one of us in our own language and switch quickly from the one to the other!

The other invitation to Tanzania was from the Rev. and Mrs. B. Marsh of the Church Missionary Society in Arusha who had a multiracial congregation in the town. It had African, European and Indian members worshipping together. Outwardly we did not see much fruit from the series of meetings, but we believe the Lord brought us there at a special time to minister to the congregation. During the meetings we met Bill Carmichael and his wife. Bill, from Ireland, was a Government Forestry Officer in the Arusha area at the time, but later entered the Church of Scotland ministry and we have kept in touch down through the years.

We also had the privilege of meeting another Irish couple at the services. John Russell was a Government Agricultural Officer in the western area of Tanzania and he and his wife had come across for the meetings. They invited us to go to their home and have a break there.

The invitation came as an answer to prayer for two reasons. Firstly, after so many months of continuous meetings, preaching and living in the cramped quarters of the van, we felt the need 'to go apart and rest awhile' as Jesus suggested to His disciples. Secondly, with many people professing conversion during the recent services, we felt very concerned about follow-up teaching for them, or as Peter expresses it, as new born babes they needed the sincere milk of the Word. Many of them were connected to small prayer houses, where the services were taken by elders who had only had a few years at school and no formal Bible training. Their ministers had twenty, thirty, and sometimes more of these prayer houses in each parish, and could only visit them very infrequently.

Because of this concern we felt the need to prepare a little book of Bible studies in simple English that could be read by those who had only been to school for three or four years, and also to make it easier for anyone who wanted to translate it into a local language. A month's stay with the Russells enabled us to pray over the matter and to put twelve simple studies on paper, to which we gave the title *Following Jesus*.

That little book has been translated into many African languages, as well as Hindustani, and although we have not been able to keep count of the numbers printed in these different languages, we estimate that they must be over the 100,000 mark. Africa Christian Press now publish the English version. By request of the Evangelical Association of Africa and Madagascar, I later expanded the book into fifty lessons for the basic text of their Theological Education by Extension Programme (TEE).

After spending the month with the Russells, we headed north to Kenya as Dr. Clive Irvine had invited us back to speak at a special conference for pastors at Chogoria, Kenya in the early part of 1957. On the way we visited the Scriptural Holiness Mission at Londiani, Kenya. I had sent a telegram to Bill Finch, who was in charge of their Mission station, with the message, 'Arriving Monday night. Selfridges.'

When we drove into the station, we found Bill standing at the door of the mission house looking anxiously at us. Coming up to our van he said, 'I did not know how to expect you.' We were surprised at his statement until he told us, 'Your telegram read, "Arriving Monday tight."' Bill and his wife Mary with her sister Miriam ran an industrial school for boys and a girls' boarding school.[1] While we were on the station we had the privilege of speaking to the students of both schools, and other friends of the Mission, before driving on to Chogoria.

It was good to renew fellowship once again with Clive and his wife Joyce, as well as other missionaries on the station. It was also a privilege to minister to the men who had lonely parishes without much fellowship with other ministers, and who appreciated the conference when they could be together. Although Chogoria is more or less on the equator, it was not too hot as it is located at quite a high altitude. In fact it is situated at the foot of Mount Kenya which has snow on its summit all the year round! The snow continues to melt during the year, feeding streams which make the surrounding gardens very fertile.

By now, Isabel and I had been married over four years and during that time we had not lived together in a house alone for two weeks! The van fitted out as a camper was our only 'home', except when we were guests of others. Isabel, especially, was beginning to feel the effects physically after the second trip of almost two years of travel over 3,000 plus miles.

We felt the time had come when, if this was the Lord's work for us to do in Africa, we should investigate the possibility of having a base to which we could retreat between our safaris. In the meantime the way opened for us to sail back to Britain from Mozambique, so we began our return journey south through Tanzania, Zambia and Malawi, calling again with contacts we had made.

---

1. Later another single missionary, Mavis Bacon, joined them. I introduced her to the Mission, as a result of her having approached me, after we spoke at a missionary meeting in Ireland, on our furlough. She wanted information about mission work where she could serve, as she felt God was calling her to Africa.

Parking the van in a garage in Limbe, Malawi, we took the train from there to Beira and sailed on 17th March on a Union Castle liner round the Cape of Good Hope. The ship docked at Cape Town for some days which gave us a chance to visit our missionary friends there and also the local people with whom I worked from 1949 to 1951.

But we had sad news while we were there. I went down to the ship one day to see if there was any mail, and was given a cable which the ship had received for us. It was to inform Isabel that her older married sister, Bessie, had died. She was the sister who had been used to lead Isabel to the Lord Jesus, so they had a very close relationship. Isabel knew that she had terminal cancer, but was looking forward to being with her in her last few weeks or months. When I returned from the ship, I had to break the news to Isabel as gently as I could, which was not easy, without breaking down myself. I had known her sister and her husband well when I was a student (that was before I knew Isabel). When she visited the Mission school she used to slip me a Penguin chocolate biscuit – a very welcome treat in those war-torn years! She also was a spiritual inspiration in my life, so I was looking forward to seeing her too.

We arrived back in Southampton in April 1957, and had a very busy furlough as we were invited to share details of the work in Africa with different prayer groups and to congregations in churches.

Within about two miles of my home in Ireland, there was a prayer-meeting every night of the week in some hall or home, and we were expected to share with each group. By the time we were due to sail again late in 1957, we were quite exhausted and laughingly said we are now going back to Africa on furlough!

9

A Temporary Base

As mentioned in the previous chapter, we felt the time had come to have a base from which we could operate. Since Malawi is in such a central position in sub-Sahara Africa, we thought we should have the base there.

It is interesting to note that in 1861 the first missionaries to that part of Africa chose to go to Malawi on the recommendation of David Livingstone. He thought that boats could sail up the Zambesi and Shire rivers to the large lake in Malawi. But because the missionaries found sixty miles of rapids on the Shire river, they had to dismantle the boat and have the sections carried up stream. Fortunately the boat, which had been built on the Clyde, had been built in sections with the intention that the missionaries put it together after it had been transported to the mouth of the Zambesi.

To begin with, the leaders of the Zambesi Mission in Malawi offered us the temporary use of one of their houses which was vacant at the time on Dombole mission station. When we were ready to sail back to Malawi late in 1957 at the beginning of our third tour, we at least knew that we had a temporary base there.

We had a little suspense when we were nearing the port of Beira in Mozambique on Christmas Eve. The Captain announced that we would all have to disembark that evening! The original plan was that we would only disembark after Christmas when we would be able to get a train to Malawi. But the new situation meant that we would have to arrange accommodation in Beira over the holiday period. We did not have cash for that purpose, so we prayed that the Lord would work things out for us. We were reminded of the question in Psalm 78:19: 'Can God furnish a table in the wilderness?' We told the Lord that we knew He could!

But we were very relieved when the Captain made another announcement. Stormy conditions at sea would prevent us getting to Beira before the port would close for the Christmas holiday. The ship would have to anchor in the bay. Our prayer for accommodation was answered in that unexpected way. We had a wonderful Christmas dinner on board and when we disembarked on Boxing Day we were given packed lunches. The Lord had provided something extra for our table! We were able to get our train to Malawi the same day. There were excess luggage charges on the train for which we had not planned. But again the Lord provided from an unexpected source. We serve a wonderful Master!

When we arrived in Malawi we collected our van from the garage where it had been stored, and travelled 100 miles north to the house which had been kindly loaned to us by the Zambesi Mission. We saw that the house had not been used for sometime. Because it was the rainy season in January, we felt the need of a fire to deal with the damp atmosphere. But we got a surprise when we lit the first fire in the bedroom – a whole hive of bees fell down the chimney and landed on the bedroom floor! We did our best to get rid of them, but we had confused bees crawling around for some time.

As the loan of the house was temporary, we had to give prayerful attention to the question of a permanent base. One encouragement we received was a letter from a missionary who had attended a ministers' retreat where I had spoken on the subject of tithing. He wrote, 'I have never tithed, but the enclosed £2.00 is my first attempt, and I would like you to accept it towards the cost of a house.'

When the people in the Mzimba area, about 300 miles north

of the house where we were staying and where we had seen many conversions in 1956, heard that we were thinking of building a base, they begged us to build in their area. They saw this as a means whereby we could still continue to help those young Christians.

As we felt that their request could be a sign from God pointing out the place of His choice for us, we decided to find out if it would be possible to get a building site there. I went to the government representative for the area and asked about the possibility of obtaining a plot on which to build. In Malawi all land was government owned, apart from a few areas of freehold which had been granted to Missions and in some cases to business agencies. All other land was leased for a limited time.

The official asked me, 'Have the Africans in this district invited you to come here?' The reason for his question was the opposition to the Federation of Rhodesia and Nyasaland which the Africans felt had been set up to allow white people to take their land. A site, therefore, could only be given if the African population in the district agreed. When I confirmed that they had begged us to set up our base there, he said that he would send my application to the office in the capital which dealt with the leasing of land.

He then said, 'I'm afraid I will have to ask you for £2.00, as that is the fee required to cover the cost of the application.' £2.00 was the exact amount sent to us by the missionary who had begun to tithe, and was the only money we had to put towards our new base.

A few weeks later we were offered a one-acre plot on the three conditions: (1) We must build a house on the plot inside two years; (2) the house must have a value of not less than £1,500; (3) we had to reply inside three weeks! To promise in less than three weeks to build such a house within two years when we had no money available for that purpose required some faith! We knew that if it was God's will for us to have the house,

He would provide the necessary finance. But how were we to be sure that it was His will to build on that particular spot?

We had to have a clear assurance from Him before we made the promise to go ahead and accept the offer. Isabel and I prayed that if it was the Lord's will for us to accept, He would give us a special sign. Without telling anyone of our prayer we asked Him to send inside two weeks £100 specially designated for a house. We asked for the two-week period to give us the third week in which to reply to the government offer.

On the eighth night, as Isabel and I were having our evening worship, we read: 'Now unto Him that is able to do exceedingly abundantly above all that we ask or think ... unto him be glory in the church by Jesus Christ' (Ephesians 3:20, 21). We both sensed that the verse was the Lord's assurance to us that He was going to answer 'exceeding abundantly'. Next morning in our mail was a letter from a young man from Ireland informing us that he felt led by the Lord to send £300 towards the building of a base. He also sent £100 to help provide money for the little book we had written for young converts, *Following Jesus*. As the Lord had answered our prayer so definitely, we notified the Government Department that we were accepting the offer of the plot and the conditions which they attached.

Of course, the gift of £300 was only a fifth of what the government said must be the value of the house. The authorities did not want a shack built! Isabel and I decided that we would not incur any debt in our building programme. We would only order materials and employ workmen as the Lord made money available.

The ant hills made by the termites contain very good clay with which to make bricks. There was a large hill in the vicinity of the acre-plot that had been leased to us and we were allowed to use the clay for our bricks. Of course, the making of the bricks was a big task and took time. Water had to be carried, mixed with the clay by the stamping of bare feet, then put into moulds and laid out for some time to dry in the sun. Then they had to be built up into the shape of a kiln with channels for fire underneath. Next wood had to be cut to fire the kiln for a number of days until the bricks were thoroughly burned.

After receiving permission to build, we knew that clearing the plot, making the bricks, getting plans passed, and the hiring of bricklayers, carpenters and the labourers would all take time. We arranged with a local African contractor to hire the men he needed to make the bricks and prepare for the building, while we dealt with getting the plans passed. Of course, we prayed for the rest of the money that would be needed to get a start made on building. But we knew the Lord had made it clear that He wanted us to build and we were confident the money would come in as it was needed.

Evangelistic Outreach from the Temporary Base

Although it was early in 1958 when we received permission to build, we knew that it would be around six months before the building could be commenced. We had found a reliable man to supervise the preparation, and that left us free to continue our evangelistic outreach from the temporary base we had, with occasional visits to the site to see how things were proceeding.

There were two areas of outreach during those months. One was invitations from a number of churches and missions in Zambia and Tanzania for special services. The trip would be a circular one of approximately 2,000 miles. The other request was for further services in the north of Malawi including a mission to students in Livingstonia Secondary School.

The details of the 2,000 mile trip had been settled and the day was drawing near for our departure, when we realised that our total finance amounted to £1.00! Our first reaction was to cancel the trip. Since the Lord had not provided sufficient funds to cover the cost of the trip, we took that to mean that it was not His will for us to go. But that conclusion raised the difficult question, What reason were we to give for the cancellation to the African pastors and missionaries who had invited us and to whom we had made the promise to help?

There were two reasons why we could not tell them of our lack of finance. First, we had promised the Lord that we would never let our personal financial position or needs be known to anyone except Himself; we felt to do otherwise would be preying on people, not praying to our Heavenly Father. Secondly, we knew that people would feel obligated to send money which had never been discussed when the arrangements were made.

The Lord provides for our travel!

So what were we to write? We had no other excuse! We went back to prayer and were impressed with a question which we sensed the Holy Spirit was asking, 'Is £1 not enough to start you off on the journey?' We had to admit that it would take us a little way! We felt then that we should start out, having faith that the Lord would provide for the rest of the mileage.

It seemed that Satan was working hard to hinder us from taking the trip, and not only over money. The afternoon before we were due to leave I had an accident while packing the van. I stepped backwards out of the van onto the edge of a stone and sprained my ankle. It was very painful and soon became badly swollen and discoloured. The condition of my ankle made it impossible for me to drive the van over the corrugated and pot-holed roads. The long distances would have been too much for Isabel to drive. It seemed as if Satan had succeeded in stopping our trip.

As usual at such times of frustration, Isabel and I went to prayer to seek the Lord's will for us. Isabel felt that the Lord reminded her of James 5:15: 'The prayer of faith shall save the sick, and the Lord shall raise him up ....' She said to me, 'I feel as if the Lord is impressing on me that I should anoint your foot with oil and pray in faith that your ankle will be healed, as there is no elder near here. The Lord knows that we are due to start tomorrow on a journey to do His work which we believe He had confirmed was His will, and it is impossible to do so with your ankle in that condition!'

I got a surprise. Of course, we had often prayed in the past for ourselves and others when sick and had seen the Lord answer in His own way and time, when it was His will. But Isabel felt that in the short time that was left before our departure the Lord could heal my ankle. I joined her in faith.

She prayed, 'Lord, you have told us in James that we should call for the elders to anoint and pray for the sick. You know that we cannot do Your work in the next few weeks unless Jack's ankle is healed. There are no church elders near us where we are just now and so we cannot ask them to pray. Please accept our faith for the healing of the ankle as I apply some oil.'

The Authorised Version of the Bible which we were using did not state the type of oil to be used, so I will not go into details about the type she used!

The pain left immediately after her prayer, the swelling went down, and the following morning the ankle was normal. We made the final arrangements for our departure and I jumped into the driving seat and had no further trouble with my ankle. I should mention that was the one and only time Isabel was led to take that action. We concluded that as it was an emergency the Lord impressed her with special instruction from His Word.

With £1's worth of petrol to start us, we began our 2,000 mile trip, a three month safari. Without telling anyone of our needs, our expenses were provided until we were back within 400 miles of our temporary base. We were back in Malawi, but we had only three pennies left!

We had been invited to stay for a few days with Dr. Ken and Elsabe Irvine at Ekwendeni Mission. As we arrived, Isabel asked me, 'What do you think we should do?' We knew that Ken and Elsabe would have helped us if they knew our position, but we had promised the Lord that we would not inform people about our needs. I could only reply, 'If the Lord does not send us some money for petrol, He must want us to stay longer and do some outreach at Ekwendeni until He provides for the rest of the journey!'

However, when we reached the Irvine home, Elsabe said, 'By the way, there is a letter here for you.' We had not given their address to anyone, so we were surprised as we had not expected any mail there. When she handed us the letter, we found from the number of re-directions on it and the postal frank that it had taken two months to reach us although it had been sent by air-mail from Ireland!

On opening the envelope, it contained a £5 postal order and a note in which the writer wrote, 'I do not know why I am sending you this postal order, but the Lord has impressed upon me that I should send it!' Well, we knew why the Lord had impressed him with that message. The Good Shepherd had fore-seen that eight weeks ahead two of his sheep would be stranded 400 miles from their fold, and through a series of addresses, He made sure that our need would be met on time! The Psalmist pointed out that when He is our Shepherd we 'shall not want', or as a little girl misquoted it, 'He's all I want'.

We don't think that any thoughtful person would say that the £5 arrived by chance when we had only three pennies left and 400 miles to travel. Especially when the letter had chased us around for two months, and just reached us in our time of need at an address about which we had not notified anyone.

When we gave the Lord His tithe, we had enough left to take us back to our base. We returned with much praise to the Lord for providing all our needs during the three months we were away.

I will detail some of the events which we experienced during those months of travel. We had a large number of services for students, elders and congregations as we travelled west in Zambia and then visited the towns on the Copperbelt. After the services there, we were invited to come back at a later date to organize three months of special training for elders in the United Church of Zambia.

From the Copperbelt we travelled north towards Tanzania on what is known as the Cape to Cairo road, having fellowship with missionaries and church leaders on the way, addressing meetings, and talking to students.

A person who claimed to have risen from the dead

I had a very unusual contact near Lubwa Mission with a woman named Alice Linshina who had become ill and 'died', at least according to her relatives and others in the village. They wrapped her body in the customary way for burial. While the grave was being dug, relatives called and the family and neighbours gathered around the body in the home to wail and show their sorrow for her passing.

During the time of mourning with its loud crying and wailing, suddenly the wrapped figure was seen to move! Although most of those around were very frightened, a few of the women managed to unwrap the body and to their surprise Alice sat upright and greeted them. What a change – the wailing had stopped and fright had taken over!

When the situation had settled down, Alice said to them, 'I have been in another country. In the far distance I saw wonderful, shining buildings and I knew that it was heaven. I started to walk towards the buildings, but then I saw someone dressed in white coming towards me. I knew He was Jesus. He asked me, "Where are you going?" I said, "I want to go to that shining city of heaven." He then said to me, "You are not ready to go there. You must go back to earth, repent of your sins, and tell the people that witchdoctors do not get their power from Me."'

Her story caused a sensation in Zambia. People from all over wanted to see this woman 'who had come back from the dead' as she claimed. Crowds began to congregate at her village. As she had been attending church classes before her illness with the object of becoming a church member, she then asked the elders of the local United Church of Zambia to allow her to explain to the congregation what she had experienced. For some reason, the details of which I have not been informed, they refused to allow her to speak in church. Because it was something they had never been asked to do before, perhaps they were afraid of what might happen. Some of them could have been afraid of revenge from the witchdoctors when she announced that they did not get their power from God!

Their reaction resulted in her not only leaving the church, but condemning it and then starting her own church! As large crowds flocked to her village, she succeeded in influencing many of them against the United church. She began to baptise them in the local river. She went on to forbid them to sing any hymns out of the local church hymnary and introduced 'hymns' of her own.

Because of her claim that she had met Jesus when she 'died' and that He was still giving her messages, people took her instructions very seriously. When she said that the Lord had told her to build a large church, tradesmen and hundreds of helpers became involved in seeing that it was erected. She went to bricklayers, carpenters and others who could assist with the building and told them that God had asked her to enlist them to do the work, and He would tell her how much to pay them! Others were informed that she was told by God to ask them for money to buy items like cement, nails and roofing. The result was that the largest 'church' in all of rural Zambia was built.

Her opposition to the established church grew to such an extent that in her preaching she associated the church with Satan and went as far as to say that anyone who killed a member of that church would receive a special passport to heaven.

When we were staying on Lubwa Mission, I felt led to visit

her to try and have a talk with her. After a long walk through the bush, I arrived and was given a seat and told to wait. I was kept waiting a long time without any excuse being given. This was not African custom, and I concluded she was hoping I would see that she was a very important person.

When she appeared, her welcome was rather cold. I asked why she had turned against the church which had brought the gospel to her district. Why had she started another 'church' in opposition? As she 'beat around the bush', and tried to justify herself in the actions she had taken, I came to the conclusion that there were three reasons why she had been led astray.

First, there was the action of the session when they seemed to ignore her desire to talk to the church about what had happened. I do not know, but if they had shown love and concern for her at that time, they might have been able with God's help to direct and guide her into a humble walk with the Lord. As a result of how she was treated, she became bitter and resentful.

Secondly, hundreds of people came from many parts of Zambia to see her and hear of her experience when she 'died', and it seemed to bolster her ego when she so suddenly became very famous. Gifts were given to her as she baptised many and made them members of her cult. As we know, pride leads a person from one precipice to another, and without spiritual advice from mature Christians, things went from bad to worse.

Thirdly, the politicians who were pressing for independence for Zambia suddenly realised that they had a wonderful asset. If they could harness Alice and her fame, attraction and organization for political purposes, they would have a wonderful weapon for furthering their ambitions. This they had managed to do to a great extent, and had drawn the wrath of the Federal Government which not only opposed the politicians of the African Congress but also proscribed the cult organization of Alice!

I did not have much outward success in talking to her. I tried to remind her of Saul. God's message to him through Samuel was that when he was little in his own eyes God blessed him, but when he became disobedient and took his own way, he was forsaken by God.

Two serious things happened shortly after my visit. The government defence forces decided to go into her village and disperse the hundreds of people who had gathered there as they felt there was a risk to security. Unfortunately the forces were attacked by the mob, bicycle chains and other implements were used against the forces, and they had to take measures to protect themselves which resulted in quite a fierce battle, with dead and wounded.

The second happening was even more serious. Followers of the Alice cult attacked some villages one night, burned down the huts and killed about 150 people. They felt they would get a better place in heaven because they had killed people who belonged to what Alice said were false churches.

Her so-called church being proscribed by government, Alice was captured and put under a type of house arrest in an area far removed from her own village and tribe. After a number of years she died while still in detention.

The injection that caused a sensation
Leaving Zambia we continued up the Cape to Cairo road to Tanzania, again visiting the Moravian mission with its large secondary school, and then going on to the Swedish Evangelistic Mission in the west of the country where the missionaries had invited us to spend a few days of rest with them.

As the last number of weeks had been very hectic we looked forward to a break, and Isabel and I decided that we would not show our medical kit or dental forceps during our stay. We knew that if we showed them, most of our time would be taken up with patients!

On the second morning of our stay as we walked out of the house we saw three men approaching. The man in the middle was being held upright by the other two. When they came nearer we noticed that the man had a very swollen neck. The helpers begged the missionary's wife to do something for the sick man, as he had not eaten for six days and had not been able to drink anything for three days! She pointed out to them that there was no nurse or doctor on the station and that they must take him to the hospital. But the hospital was fifty miles away and they said the sun was too hot to carry him during the day and the lions made it too dangerous to take him at night. There was no bus for some days.

The missionary's wife, knowing that Isabel was a nurse and I had had a little medical training, asked us if we could help. We looked at one another, remembering that it was best not to get involved with patients if we wanted a little rest! However, a couple of days could be fatal, so we agreed to help. All we had was a sulphur drug for intestinal troubles. We thought the tablets might do some good, but then we remembered that he could not swallow! I suggested that we dissolve a couple of tablets in sterile water and give an intermuscular injection. Isabel reluctantly agreed, so after praying we gave him an injection, but urged him to go to the hospital on the first bus! I must admit that I thought if the Lord used the injection to keep him alive until then it would be wonderful.

The next day we had a great surprise! One of the friends, who had been with him the previous day, came running to the Mission Station, exclaiming that his friend was now alright, he was drinking and eating well! (On relating this incident later to Dr. Clive Irvine at Chogoria, he said, 'Jack, I'm convinced that it was more your prayers than the injection which resulted in his healing!')

But the people in the surrounding villages did not think it was only prayer. The following morning when we came out of the little hut in which we were sleeping, we found many people sitting around the station yard. During breakfast I asked the missionary if he had a special meeting arranged for that day.

'No,' he replied, looking puzzled, 'why do you ask?' I then told him that we had seen many people gathered in the yard. He asked his son to go and find out the reason for their coming. When he returned, his son smiled, before announcing to his father: 'They have heard that there is a new doctor and nurse on the station who can give "powerful" injections, so they have all come for help!'

From that day until we left the mission station, we had many patients each day with various ailments. One, for instance, came with the top of his thumb almost completely severed and asked us to sew it. When we enquired how the accident had occurred, he was very reluctant to tell us, but when we refused to help him until he explained, he gave the following account through an interpreter:

'When my wife and I were sleeping in our hut last night, some goats broke down the grass door and entered the hut. I asked my wife to get up and put out the goats and close the door. She refused and said, "You are the one who closed the door, so you should get up to attend to the goats." Then we began to argue, and very soon it came to blows, and during the fight she bit the top off my thumb.'

We informed him that we could stitch his thumb, but we could not take the anger out of their hearts. Only Jesus the great Doctor could do that, so it gave us an opportunity to give all the waiting patients a talk on salvation. As we had to leave soon afterwards the missionary's wife removed the stitches later.

Our worst experience of thirst

When we were ready to leave western Tanzania for our journey back through Zambia to Malawi, we were informed that we could take a route that would cut off many miles of the trip south. It was the time of the year which is known as the dry season in that part of Africa when there are no rain storms. A large section of Tanzania which is a swamp in the rainy season had a dry cracked surface over which vehicles could pass. We decided to take the short-cut, but were not told that mosquitoes worked their 'malarial' night-shift there and the tsetse flies took over the 'sleeping sickness' shift during the day.

We started our journey during the day and soon found the tsetses flying in through the open windows of the van. We were quite badly bitten before we managed to close the windows. As they were sliding ones, many flies still squeezed in to the van between the panes of glass.

Because of the intense tropical heat in the van with the windows closed, it was not long before we had consumed all our drinking water, and we looked anxiously for a water hole as we travelled. We had never been so thirsty, as mile after mile passed without any sign of water. Eventually we did see a water hole in the distance, beside what we thought was a large rock. However, as we approached, we found that the 'rock' was an elephant! Naturally we left the elephant to enjoy the water, knowing how dangerous it could be if disturbed, but seeing the water and an animal enjoying it only made us more thirsty.

We kept driving until late in the afternoon when we came to a very muddy stream. We stopped, boiled some of the water and added tea so that we would not see its colour, and we drank and drank. Never did tea taste so good! I have often used this incident in sermons to illustrate the thirst of the soul which David mentions in Psalm 42:2: 'My soul thirsteth for God', and how so many are trying to quench that soul thirst from the sinful 'broken cisterns that can hold no water' (Jeremiah 2:13). The only way in which soul thirst can be quenched is not by drugs, alcohol or other sinful pleasures, but by Jesus: 'Whosoever drinketh of the water that I shall give him, shall never thirst' (John 4:14).

After enjoying the muddy tea, we travelled on to the next government station and met the doctor there. When he heard that we had been bitten by tsetse flies, he was quite concerned because of the danger of 'sleeping sickness'. He urged us to be sure to seek medical help if we discovered symptoms like severe headaches. Fortunately, that was not necessary, so we could only thank the Lord for His protection.

We reached Malawi around the middle of 1958 and arrived at the home of Ken and Elsabe Irvine, where as I have already mentioned, the Lord provided money for the 400 miles back to our base, when we had only three pence left.

As it can be imagined, the travelling on the very dusty roads was not very pleasant. As Isabel wrote once, 'I recall one day being so fed-up with all the dust pouring in through the windows which had to be kept open because of the heat. It seemed to get into everything in the van. There was no air-conditioning in our "house on wheels". Then we were reminded that we should be thankful because when David Livingstone travelled over those parts, he had no vehicle, but had to walk!'

10

Building Our New Base

By September 1958 the plot was cleared, the bricks were ready, some cement had been delivered, and bricklayers and labourers had been hired by the man we made responsible, and so it was time to measure and lay out the plan for the foundation. The Lord had provided enough money to make a start and also to obtain materials which were needed immediately.

We felt that we should then leave the temporary base and move to the plot and camp in our tent there, and so keep up to date with the work as well as seeing that materials were there when needed.

It was not our intention to stay on the site all the time, though. We had invitations to help with evangelistic outreach in the north of Malawi. A bricklayer who had been trained by the government works' department had been hired, and we felt he could keep things going during our spells away.

More village meetings

As the roads up into the hills were not suitable for vehicles it was decided that our first series of meetings should be held at a village near the main road. Villagers from the hills could come down and meet there. In fact many hundreds attended and gave us a very warm welcome. Isabel describes the reception:

'When we were having services and doing medical and dental work in the villages, the people were very friendly, especially the Christians. We were given eggs, chickens, rice, maize and honey. Even old women would come and hand us pennies, saying it would help us to buy petrol!

'At this village we had an unforgettable time. We were given nine dozen eggs and seventeen fowl during the weekend we were there. I suggested to the people that we have a feast for all who had gathered, using the gifts the people had brought as we had no space to carry the fowl. I had no intention of putting them into the van as they had fleas. The villagers refused, saying they could not eat gifts they had given to us! They suggested that they would make a large coop with local twigs and put it on top of the van!

'They proceeded to do so, and after pushing the fowl into the coop, some strong men hauled the caged birds up on to the top of the van. Our van became a double-decker and we drove away with the fowl on the top deck!'

We knew that there would be more chickens waiting for us at the next village where we were due to preach! What were we to do? We could not feed the chickens, they were too heavy to lift down at feeding time. However, we found a solution.

Our van needed some mechanical attention and we stopped at a government roads' department workshop. The mechanic was glad to examine the van and do what he could to deal with the trouble. While I was with him in the workshop, Isabel was invited into their house by his wife. Isabel reports about their conversation:

'I asked her if she had any chickens. She replied, "No. I do not keep chickens, but I sometimes send my house-servant out to the villages to try and buy one for cooking, but he usually returns saying that none of the villagers wanted to sell chickens or eggs." I then asked if she would like to have seventeen chickens and nine dozen eggs, explaining to her how we received them and that we had no way of handling them. She was delighted to accept them and gave us money which she said we could use to buy other items of food.' Just as we expected, six chickens and some eggs were waiting for us at our next preaching location.

After the meetings there, we were invited to hold services at a Mission Station high up in the Misuku hills in the north of Malawi on the border with Tanzania. The mission was situated thirty-five miles from the main road and our two-wheel-drive vehicle could not cope with the steep mountainous tract leading up to the station. The missionary had to come down with his four-wheel-drive vehicle and use its winch to pull us up some nasty parts of the track.

The Christians in the churches there appreciated the services very much. They did not see visiting preachers often because of the very difficult approach and they were glad to have an opportunity of evangelistic gatherings where they could invite people who did not usually come to church. The Lord blessed us with a spiritually fruitful week.

We did not know at the time that difficult days were ahead for the missionary and his wife as well as the Christians on the station. When a state of emergency was declared in the country in 1959 (described in a later chapter) and rioting broke out, a man who was a friend of the missionary came rushing to the station and informed him: 'I have just come from a political meeting where it was decided that you and your wife are to be killed. You must get away now. Don't delay.'

The missionary took his advice. He and his wife packed a few of their most valuable things into the vehicle quickly and drove down the hillside. An observation plane which flew over the station soon after found that all the buildings had been burned to the ground. The quick reaction of that man informing the missionary no doubt saved their lives.

It seemed that the Lord had arranged our visit to help strengthen the Christians for the trying days ahead from Communistic driven anti-Christian violence which also robbed them of their missionaries.

Our meetings came to an end and it was time for us to start our journey down the escarpment. It was hair-raising as the van leaned over at dangerous angles going round corners. By the time we got down safely and then travelled the long distance to the next village it was becoming dark.

The village was in Zambia. Because it was difficult to reach the village from other parts of Zambia, the church became a congregation of the Livingstonia Synod in Malawi. Again I will hand over to Isabel and copy from a report she wrote on the subject, *Life with Jack*.

'When we reached the village, we got the usual warm welcome from the minister and the members of the congregation as well as the other villagers. Before going to bed, I decided to make a cup of tea. What a shock I had on opening the door of the cupboard in which we kept our food! To my horror I discovered that a tin of treacle on the top shelf had fallen over and the lid had come loose, perhaps because of heat. The heat also caused the treacle to flow down through the cupboard over the food on the lower shelves and into drawers where we kept bed linen and personal clothes, ending up in our shoes underneath the cupboard!

'My first reaction was to sit down and cry. It was too late to do anything about the problem that night. Somehow we got to bed eventually, with the big question on my mind, how was I to get rid of those treacle stains?

'The next day, between our services, I spent a long time cleaning up as well as washing the linen in a small basin. It was a number of weeks before I got rid of all the treacle stains! That was the last time we had treacle in the van, even though Jack was very fond of it. But in spite of the treacle problem, the Lord blessed the services and a number of people were convicted for sin and sought the Lord's forgiveness and salvation, and Christians were drawn to deeper commitment.'

By the time we returned to the plot again the workmen had started building the walls. An amusing incident happened one day when I was having a look around at the work. I could see that a wall which had been built up to four feet was out of plumb. I asked the bricklayer to check it and he was surprised to see that it was out four inches. He looked at me and said, 'You have a good eye!' I found he was more careful to depend on his plumb line and spirit-level after that.

A Trial of Faith

The Lord provided what was needed for the building work until the house was nearing roof level. We had paid our bills up-to-date for materials and also the wages of the workmen. But then our funds run out and we needed materials for roofing and wages for the hiring of a carpenter to fit it.

There had been times before when we had reached the end of our resources. However, we found that those times were allowed by our kind heavenly Father to enable us to stretch our faith and confidence in Him and see the wonderful, miraculous ways in which He was able to provide.

I remember one day, when out walking, having a 'conversation' with the Lord. I said, 'Lord, why do You not always see that provision is made ahead of time for our needs, so that we do not have to come and ask You to supply?' I then felt the Lord was asking me a question, 'When you have a need and come to Me and ask and I supply that need, what effect does it have on you?'

I answered, 'It gives us great joy and assurance of Your power and loving care, causing us to praise and thank You.'

'That is why I do it that way, it increases faith and produces praise,' I felt the Lord respond.

John Bunyan said, 'I shovel out to God, and He shovels back to me, but His shovel is bigger than mine!' How often we proved that to be true, and also the words of the Lord Jesus true when He said: 'Give, and it shall be given unto you; good measure, pressed down, and shaken together, and running over, shall men give into your bosom!' (Luke 6:38).

Not only were funds needed to continue the building of the house, we also were unable to buy some items of food we felt were necessary. As the days passed and no money was received, Satan took advantage of the situation to suggest that somewhere we had made a mistake and God was displeased with us and not supplying our needs.

After some days we felt that the position could not continue. We could not have faith with such a question mark in our minds. It had to be settled one way or the other. Either the Lord was displeased or He was withholding funds for a reason known only to Himself. We had to have an answer. As we prayed we knew that it was not like our kind heavenly Father to punish us without telling us why, so we concluded that it was Satan who was making such suggestions. We remembered Job and how Satan tried to take advantage of him when the Lord had allowed circumstances to come about so that He could get the glory.

We told the Lord that we were trusting Him to provide, but asked, 'Lord, if You are still pleased with us, would You send us a little token of Your love today? It does not matter how small it is, but it would strengthen our faith to know that You will provide all we need to finish the house and help us to overcome Satan's suggestions'.

We thought that the Lord would send a postal order as He had done at other times. Therefore I said to Isabel, 'I am going down to the post office on our little autocycle to collect our mail and on my way back I will blow the horn to let you know that the Lord has answered.' I was so sure that the Lord would answer, but I was expecting Him to do it in my way.

There was no letter for us in the post office! I returned rather slowly, with no horn sounding, and I found Isabel in tears as it looked as if Satan was correct! But we joined in prayer again and reminded the Lord that the day was not over and we were still expecting Him to answer.

We found that the Lord's ways are not our ways. He had

other methods apart from postal orders. He loves to take us out of ruts! In fact we are convinced that the Lord has a wonderful sense of humour!

A little later, a landrover pulled up in front of our tent, and the driver handed us a cardboard box saying, 'Elsabe Irvine asked me to leave this with you.' When we opened the box, we found bread, a cooked chicken, a cake and other groceries! If we had received a postal order we would have had to go about 180 miles to buy some of the items in the box! The Lord is very good at business decisions. He provided a 'Table in the wilderness' (Psalm 78:19).

That experience taught us two wonderful lessons which have proved very valuable to us many times since then. First, we do not need to retain a question mark in our minds. Jesus said, 'If any man will do his will, he shall know of the doctrine, whether it be of God...' (John 7:17). Paul wrote, 'Be ye not unwise, but understanding what the will of the Lord is' (Ephesians 5:17).

Second, God does not work in ruts. We are warned not to 'limit the Holy One of Israel', as the Israelites did (Psalm 78:41). We can limit Him by expecting Him to work in the same way as He worked in the past. After the Lord had answered our prayers in His way, we were enabled to step out afresh in faith, knowing that He would supply all our needs.

Gifts arrived from many sources – churches, prayer groups, mission halls and individuals. But special mention must go to a prayer group in my own village in Northern Ireland. Mrs. Jean Fleming, who went to heaven in 1994, suggested to the weekly Prayer Union group in the village that they take responsibility to provide the money for the roof of the house, as I had been a member of the prayer group before I left home for training.

Not only did they provide the necessary money for the roof timbers and asbestos sheets[1], but from that time in 1958 until

---

1. Asbestos was used for roofing in those days, as it was cooler in the tropical heat.

1986 when we reached mission retirement age, they continued to support our evangelistic work.

We had accepted an invitation from the Rev. Bill Hincks, a Canadian who was evangelism secretary for the United Church of Zambia on the Copperbelt, to conduct evangelistic meetings in all the main towns there from November 1958 to January 1959. The building of the house was taking longer than expected. Only one room had been roofed as the time drew near for us to leave. As the house had no doors it could not be locked. In addition the builders still needed some items to be purchased. Reluctantly we felt that the only solution was for us to separate. I would leave for the services in Zambia and Isabel would remain at the plot and do all she could to speed up the completion of the house.

Three months of separation

It was very hard for me to leave Isabel alone. The nearest missionaries were thirty miles away and she did not have any transport except a little moped. There was only one room with a roof, but it had no ceiling, and there were no doors fitted on the house, so at night she had to prop up a sheet of asbestos to close off her bedroom – not a very secure way to keep out human visitors, animals, snakes and other nocturnal wanderers in an African night!

Elsabe Irvine came down for a few days of fellowship with Isabel. A second room had been roofed in the meantime, but there were still no doors fitted, so Elsabe had to use a sheet of asbestos as a door for the second bedroom as well. The rooms had no ceilings, so Isabel and Elsabe were able to carry on conversations after they had gone to bed in their respective rooms! Isabel appreciated Elsabe's stay.

I was over 700 miles away in the Copperbelt. I had taken with me two of the teenage boys who had professed faith in Christ during the special meetings we had in Mzimba in 1956.

The meetings in the seven towns in Zambia were very much appreciated by the local Christians. Services were very well attended and many expressed their desire to turn to Christ and forsake their sinful ways. It can be imagined how much temptation there was for those who left their tribal areas and had come into the towns to find work in the copper mines. With tribal culture broken down, it was easy to get involved in beer-drinking and immorality. Beer was brewed locally from maize and the brewers' adverts claimed it was very nourishing! But it was also intoxicating as it was consumed in great quantities in beer-gardens.

I was in the middle of the last week of the three months of meetings when I received a cable which stated: '*Isabel very ill. Return immediately.*'

Although I was able to cancel the rest of the meetings, for me to get 'immediately' to Isabel was a problem. Driving non-stop the journey would take over twenty-four hours and there were a number of difficulties in trying to do it that quickly. Obviously, there was the danger of falling asleep at the wheel. But also January was the middle of the rainy season when the slippery, clay roads made it dangerous to drive very fast. Furthermore, petrol was not obtainable at night on the road.

Another problem was that a 100-mile stretch of the journey was a very narrow, mountainous part of the road. On that stretch, heavy traffic was only allowed to go west during certain hours and east at a different time. As my van was a 25 cwt. model it was not classed as a heavy vehicle, so I could enter the one-way area at any time. But it was very dangerous to do so when the heavy traffic was coming in the opposite direction! The drivers felt they had the right of way and usually travelled faster than they should! If I left immediately, I would enter that stretch of road at the wrong time.

To go by bus would have meant changing buses three or four times, with long delays at bus stations; to go by air would also have meant three or four different planes with no assurance of connections. I had thought of hiring a small plane, but that was beyond my financial ability. The journey in my own van was the only solution, even though I would not arrive 'immediately'.

I started off at 3.00 pm. On the first part of the journey I travelled south to Lusaka which was not too difficult as the road was fully tarred. From there I branched east on 350 miles of muddy clay and gravel roads to the next town, Fort Jameson.

Darkness had fallen before I had travelled very far, and with animals roaming on Africa's unfenced roads at night a constant sharp outlook was necessary. Eventually I reached the entrance to the hundred-mile stretch of road reserved for one-way traffic at the time when traffic was just entering the opposite end.

As it was around 3.00 am, I had to wake the man in charge of the barrier. He was not pleased. Looking at my van he said in broken English, 'You no go, gari-moto too big. You wait seven tomorrow.'

I explained that my van was a 25 cwt. van, and vehicles under 30 cwt. were allowed by law to enter any time. He just kept saying, 'You no go. You no go.' I then took my driver's manual and showed him the weight of the van, but he could not read! I tried to explain to him that my wife was very ill and I must drive all night to get to her, but as I did not know his language and he did not know mine, I had no success with my arguments. In my frustration I opened the barrier myself, drove through, closed it behind me and headed off east. I knew that if the guard reported me, I was allowed by law to travel and could explain to police that he misunderstood the weight of my van.

With concern for Isabel, and not knowing details of her illness, it was a very long journey. A few miles before reaching the next town, my brakes ceased to function. I thought I had allowed the brake fluid to get low, so I nursed the van the remainder of the way to the town, using the hand brake when necessary. I found a garage and asked to have the van's brake system replenished with fluid. While that was being done, I decided to try and phone the police at Mzimba, as they would know of Isabel's condition.

'I am afraid I have bad news for you.'

I found a phone kiosk and asked the operator to put me through to the police in Mzimba. The operator had to route the call through the three capitals of Zambia, what is now Zimbabwe and Malawi before getting through to Mzimba in the north of Malawi. The operator came back on to my line to tell me that she could not get through to the police. I then asked her to try the magistrate, knowing that in the small village of Mzimba, the news of Isabel's illness would be known to all the government people who had offices there. Again I got the same reply, 'Sorry, I cannot get through.'

As a last resort, I asked for the Mzimba hospital. While I was holding the phone in the kiosk, hoping the operator would get through at the third attempt, I saw her leaving the exchange and coming towards me. I thought that was very strange! Something must be wrong! When she reached the kiosk, she said, 'I am afraid I have bad news for you.'

I felt myself getting very weak for I expected her next words to be, 'Your wife has passed away!' However, she quickly added, 'The lines are down.' She must have seen by my face that I was in danger of passing out with shock. Then she realised the meaning I had first taken from her message. 'Go off to the hotel and get yourself a cup of tea,' she said, 'and I will continue to try and contact Mzimba, and if I have success, I will contact the hotel.'

'No,' I said, 'I will just start off for home as I do not want to waste any more time.'

I still had about 200 miles of my journey left on rough, pot-holed, clay roads, so I rushed back to the garage to collect my vehicle. Another surprise awaited me there. The manager said, 'Sorry, your van is not ready. We discovered that one of the fluid pipes to the back wheels was ruptured. That is why you lost your fluid and we have had to take it off to braze it, so you will need to take a seat and wait for it.'

While waiting, I was sorry that the operator did not know of the delay as she could have contacted me there at the garage if she had any success with a call. I then asked the manager if I could please phone the telephone exchange as my wife was very ill and a message could come through for me there. He readily agreed.

As soon as I got through to the operator she said, 'I'm so glad you phoned. I did not know where to contact you. I was able to get through to Mzimba and I was told that your wife is a little better.' What a relief, and answer to prayer! I said I would stop on my way out and pay for the calls, but she told me there would be no charge.

I started off with a lighter heart which helped me to overcome the feeling of tiredness after all the hours of driving. I arrived home later that afternoon and received a warm welcome from Isabel who was very glad that I had returned early. I was then able to gather together some of the details of what had happened.

She had taken ill with malaria for which the doctor had treated her. In the meantime she had received a message that her mother had died in Scotland on the 31st of December. That was only five months after her father's death. Isabel's condition then had deteriorated and she was losing consciousness, so the local government doctor suspected that she had cerebral malaria. The mission doctor, Ken Irvine, also came to see her and it was decided to send the cable for me to return immediately. The government doctor went the thirty miles to the nearest mission station at Loudon and brought one of the single ladies, Jessie Campbell, to stay with Isabel until I returned. However, the doctor discovered in the meantime that Isabel was allergic to the medicine which he had prescribed for malaria and it was causing the cerebral symptoms. From the time he changed her medicine, she began to recover. We praised the Lord together.

The building of the house had continued well while I was away and so I was able to concentrate on the finishing details. Doors had to be fitted, painting and decorating had to be done, and a hot water system designed. We had a wood burning, cooking stove with a water boiler sent out from Scotland. With the use of two forty-four-gallon drums in the attic, one as a feeder tank for cold water to the system and the other for the hot water, we were able to have a circuit. The cold water had to be pumped into the drum manually as there was no piped water supply.

As the house was progressing, the political situation in Malawi was deteriorating. Most of the Africans in the three countries in the Federation of Rhodesia and Nyasaland were against the imposition of the Federation and we found ourselves affected by the unrest.

11

Nyasaland Declares An Emergency

Dr. Hastings M. Banda arrived in Malawi 1958 during the time our house was being built. He had been called back from Ghana, where he was practising medicine, to lead the Nyasaland African Congress.

The following year, anti-government boycotts, stone-throwing at white people's cars and other methods of civil disobedience were introduced of which advantage was taken by some to cause public danger.

The chief government officer in our area came to see me and said, 'There is going to be trouble here. According to our intelligence service, we are expecting rioting and have decided to bring all white women into the government centre where they will be protected by the army. Will you arrange for your wife to come?'

I replied, 'I will ask her, but I think that she will refuse.' I was correct. She felt that as the Lord had placed us in our house by invitation of the Africans, it would not be a good witness to them if she depended on guns to protect her. Also it would look as if we were involved in the political side of the unrest.

Soon afterwards the Federal Government declared a State of Emergency in the country and the Nyasaland African Congress was banned on the 3rd of March, 1959. Early that morning, during the hours of darkness, many hundreds of the Congress officials were rounded up and detained, including Dr. Banda. A number were wounded and some died resisting arrest. From that day rioting increased. Trees were cut down across the roads, cars were attacked, and £8,000 worth of damage was done to shops owned by Asians in our village of Mzimba.

Missionaries of the Church of Scotland on our nearest mission station in Loudon were attacked and had to flee for their lives, due to a misunderstanding. Police called at the house of the missionary-in-charge during the night to report that arrests were being made of some of the local officials of the Congress Party. Next morning, seeing the tracks of the police landrovers leading to the missionary's house, people concluded that the missionary had gone with the police to show them where the officials lived and help to make arrests, which was not true! When the missionaries had escaped by a track through the bush, as the main road into the station had been blocked to hinder their escape, the mob attacked the mission offices, chopped typewriters and other office equipment with axes, scattered files over the floor and marked in chalk on the walls, 'Freedom'.

When reports reached us during the day, we realised that when darkness fell, we could be in danger of an attack as we lived on the border of the village surrounded by thick bush. Isabel and I, with Harry Scott, who had recently arrived to do evangelistic work with us, decided that we would set up our amplifying system with the speaker at the front of our house and the microphone inside. Our plan was to sing the hymn 'What a Friend we have in Jesus' if we were attacked. Then we engaged in prayer, claiming the promise, 'When the enemy shall come in like a flood, the Spirit of the Lord shall lift up a standard against him' (Isaiah 59.19).

We were not attacked and only found out about six weeks later why that did not happen. One of the African teachers from the local primary school who had been very ill, came out of hospital and we invited him to come and spend a few days with us so that he could convalesce, as he had quite a small house and a number of children.

'I am going to tell you something,' he confided one day when he was with us, 'I did not want to tell you earlier in case you became frightened. On the night of the 3rd of March, a large group of men, mostly strangers in this area and so did not know you, came to the village to attack the airfield, but they found that Federal soldiers had landed and were guarding the field. The group then gathered in the bushes behind your house so they could decide what to do. The leader suggested that as there was a white man who lived nearby, they should attack the house. One young man in the group, who worked in the hospital and had seen you visiting there, spoke up for you both. He told how you brought things like ice-cold water and items of food to African patients, as well as the other work that you and your wife were doing. The majority of the group felt that it would be wrong to attack you and the leader was told that if he broke a pane of glass in your house he would be killed! They called off the attack.'

Soon after we received a letter from a prayer group in Guernsey which stated, 'We do not know why, but on the 3rd March we had a great burden for you in our prayer meeting and spent time praying for you.' We knew why and were able to write and tell them of the attack which had been called off at the last minute!

There was one other time when we were in danger and the Lord laid a burden of prayer on a group in Belfast, Northern Ireland. I will just mention it here although it did not happen in Malawi but in Tanzania. We had been travelling for some days and felt the need of a break. We were stopped by the side of the road looking at our map for a suitable place to camp when a European coffee farmer stopped alongside our van. On hearing that we were looking for a camping site, he offered us a place on his farm, which we accepted. He lived alone on the farm.

However, during the weekend he became very drunk and when he got Isabel alone he began to make advances to her. He assured her that he had a gun and that he would be able to deal with me. I had gone for a short walk at the time and when I returned I found Isabel in a nervous state as she narrated what had transpired. We knew that it would be very dangerous to sleep there for another night and that we should drive away. But we had one problem, some of our luggage was stored in his house. I decided to stalk back to the house in the dark, without a torch, so that I would not be spotted and become the target for a shot.

I managed to get into the house, rescue our luggage and get it back to the van without being observed. When we were packed and ready to leave, we could hear his footsteps around the van and decided to move off immediately, but the van would not start! There we were with this drunk man walking around who if he had his gun with him could easily have blown a tyre. We prayed earnestly that the engine would start and I suppose it was only a short time until it did, but under the circumstances it felt long! We drove out of the farmyard as fast as we could, wondering if a shot would follow us.

A few weeks later a letter reached us from the group in Belfast stating that as they prayed one evening they were very burdened for us and felt that we were in some danger. That was the night when I was in danger of being shot and Isabel abducted! How wonderful is the God we serve, burdening his servants to pray in times of danger.

The account recorded in the first chapter of this book when I was threatened with death in the pulpit took place during the time of the emergency in Malawi. We continued to visit the villages around our base, seeking to spread the good news of salvation in the midst of the political unrest. We were told that it was very risky as there were many troublemakers, who were seeking to show their dislike for the Federation and the emergency. One missionary who went to the government official to ask if it was alright to go out into the district was told not to go. Of course the official did not want to take responsibility for agreeing in case something happened to him. We did not ask, but continued to go out to preach as we did previously. But one night I had an unpleasant experience, soon after the attack in the church.

Threatened with Fire

I was invited by a church elder to spend a few days in his village which was about 40 miles from our house, so that we could do some outreach together to non-Christians. I was to sleep in the small thatched, mud-and-wattle house with the family of the elder. The first night I was there, suddenly all around the house there were shouts for the white man to get out and leave the village. The political youth league was surrounding the house and they were threatening to burn it down if I did not leave. They said they had been told not to allow any white person to come to their village.

That instruction had been given because the African politicians were afraid that agents of the Federal Government would be coming around with propaganda to try and persuade the villagers to vote for the Federation of the three countries and not independence. Also some of the politicians had come under the influence of communism when they went out of the country for their university education. They were not friendly to missionaries, holding the theory that 'religion is the dope of the people' and is just introduced in a country to program people to accept white ownership of land. Although the instruction not to allow white people in the villages really applied to white politicians, the youth league included me in the ban.

In a short time the local chief arrived at the house and begged me not to leave, saying that although the young people wanted to take control of the area, he must maintain his authority as he was the one who had the power to say who could enter the village. He told the young people to leave me alone, but they paid no attention to his orders and the commotion outside the house increased. I then called the chief back into the house and informed him that I had decided to leave, as I believed the young people were determined to burn down the house. I was not afraid, I told him, but I did not want to see the elder lose his house and all he had in the fire. I then said to the chief: 'If you can sort out this matter with the youth league overnight and let me know tomorrow, I will return immediately, but my being here now is making it difficult for you to reason with them.'

He agreed and I went back the forty miles to our base. The next day, I received a letter with the following message from the chief: 'Please come back, the position has been explained to the youth league. They now understand that you are not involved in any way in federal politics and that you came to give us the messages about God and the Lord Jesus Christ.' I returned to the elder's house that day and spent a week preaching and visiting without any trouble.

After these attacks in the church and village I had a visit from the Provincial Commissioner, the senior British government official. He thanked me for not allowing the police to pursue the matter as he felt that the prosecution of the offenders would only have added fuel to the rioters' actions. He knew that the troublemakers had a strange complex attitude fuelling their efforts to get independence for the country. They wanted to go to prison because that showed that they had fought for their country and made them heroes in the eyes of the local politicians! In fact, when they came out of prison they wore a type of gown with the letters P.G embroidered on the back – standing for Prison Graduate!

After these episodes with political activists, I realised that it would be very easy for something serious to happen one day, so I decided to talk to the District Secretary of the Malawi Congress Party. (The Nyasaland Congress Party had been banned when the emergency was introduced, so as the leaders wanted the new name of the country to be Malawi, a new Congress Party had been formed.) I knew the secretary well. Before the emergency he worked in the local grocery shop and attended church, but as he was also a member of the old Nyasaland Congress, he was arrested and detained on the morning when the emergency was declared. From his own account, he was very badly treated by federal soldiers during his imprisonment and when he was released he felt very bitter against the Federal Government.

Having known him personally, it was easy to remind him that I was a servant of God sent to Malawi with the good news of God's love and salvation, and that I was not involved in politics. I asked him if he would give me a letter stating that he knew me and that the Congress had no objection to me preaching the gospel. I could then show the letter to anyone who questioned my purpose in being in the villages or travelling on the road. The letter on official Malawi Congress Party letterhead read as follows:

To: Branch Secretaries in Mzimba District of Malawi Congress Party
This is to certify that Mr. Selfridge is the religious leader of Evangelism which is the same as the Church of Scotland and his job is to preach the gospel of God.

Please, when you see this letter give him no trouble at all, he is there for God's work, do not stop him. He has seen us here at the District Office, Mzimba, and you can trust us that his mission is not political.

We know him well and he is staying here at Mzimba.

Let him do church meetings without trouble and remember Ngwazi Kamuzu[1] says, 'Peace and calm.'

Signed by the District Secretary

---

1. Ngwazi Kumuzu were the names given to Dr. Banda in the local language – Ngwazi, hero, and Kamuzu, because it was stated that his mother could not conceive until she was treated by the root of a plant of that name.

After receiving the letter, I showed it at roadblocks in the villages, where the youth leaguers examined every vehicle. The excuse was to find out if the driver was carrying arms, but the young people often, out of curiosity, took advantage to search through all the personal luggage. On showing the letter at these blocks we were usually waved on and never molested again, except on one occasion. It was an amusing incident. When we had presented the letter and were not waved on, it was evident that the leader of the group wanted to ransack the contents of our van, for he opened the door and came into the van. When he was inside I asked the others in a loud voice so that he could hear me, 'Is the leader not able to read English?' He heard me and coming out of the van quickly told me to go on with my journey. I had touched a sensitive point with him because showing no respect for the letter could have implied that he had not been to school and so could not read the contents. That impression before his group was too humiliating for him to face!

The emergency lasted about four years. In 1962, it was evident to those in charge that the Federation of Rhodesia and Nyasaland could not continue with such opposition coming from all of the three countries involved. It was agreed that Nyasaland and Northern Rhodesia (renamed Malawi and Zambia by the local politicians) could have elections, but Southern Rhodesia under Ian Smith at that time did not want one-man-one-vote.

Although the Malawi Congress Party won the election in 1962 and Dr. Banda became Prime Minister, he decided that the country should remain as a British Protectorate and that the British Governor should continue to be head of government. At the time we did not know why that decision had been made by Dr. Banda, but it became evident afterwards when there was a rebellion in his cabinet over the issue of communism. Dr. Banda trained as a medical doctor in America and Edinburgh, and had actually become an elder of the Church of Scotland when he was in Edinburgh. He was not like some other African leaders who were willing to receive aid from the USSR or China and fulfil conditions attached to receiving such aid.

When he became Prime Minister, he knew that a number of the ministers in his cabinet had been trained in universities and colleges which propagated communism. Yet they were the men who had invited him back to Malawi to take charge of the party, so he was in a precarious position. When China offered £19,000,000 to the new government, Dr. Banda was not willing to accept it as he knew that the conditions attached opened the door wide to communistic propaganda and would make it difficult for him to govern as he wanted.

A number of his ministers disagreed with him. They felt the money should be accepted and then the country would be in a better position to rid itself of British civil servants and give more positions to Africans. But Dr. Banda said that no African in Malawi would replace a white person until he had the same qualifications as the person he was replacing. That split the cabinet of eight ministers, resulting in Dr. Banda dismissing three and three others resigned. He was then left with two ministers!

Dr. Banda then reported to the Governor and asked to resign as Prime Minister, but the Governor suggested that he go to parliament and ask for a vote of confidence, which he received. He was then able to choose his new cabinet without men to whom he was obligated. Dr. Banda had decided to retain the Governor because if trouble broke out in the country, the Governor could use British soldiers.

After the new cabinet had been installed, Dr. Banda declared the country a republic and he was voted in by parliament as its first President in 1964. By that time the country had settled down and Dr. Banda emphasised that 'peace and calm' must be maintained. Dr. Banda later became Life President and unfortunately, as has been evident from the recent history of Malawi, he became very dictatorial until he was replaced in 1994.

I must point out though, that during the years from the time the emergency was declared until 1964, we were free to travel around the country and continue with evangelism, conferences and seminars, seeing people accepting Jesus as Saviour and Lord, and Christians being revived.

12

The Trials of Travel

One of the invitations that came at that time was from South Africa. I was asked to conduct six weeks of meetings in different towns for the Church of the Nazarene. We accepted the invitation, and the 1,500 mile trip to Johannesburg was an eventful one.

First, we were tested again over finance! We only had enough money to cover our expenses for the first few hundred miles, but felt again that it was the Lord's will for us to start and trust Him to supply as the need arose. Our first stop was in Blantyre in the southern region of Malawi, 400 miles south of Mzimba. We spent a weekend there trusting the Lord to provide for the rest of the journey as our funds were too low to proceed.

I had an unexpected invitation to preach in an interdenominational service on Sunday evening. The minister in charge knew nothing of our financial situation, but he surprised us during his intimations when he said: 'The offering which will be given tonight will go to the Selfridges to help them on their journey!' We estimated that the gift we received was enough to pay for our petrol and food on the remaining 1,100 miles! We praised the Lord for that wonderful provision.

However, the next day on our way through Mozambique our faith was tested again. An engine mounting broke, as the clay roads in that territory at the time were atrocious. We had to proceed slowly the rest of the way to Salisbury, now Harare in Zimbabwe. Knowing that the amount of money we had was just sufficient to take us to South Africa, we were apprehensive about the cost of repairs as we went to a garage for an estimate.

I was pleased when the welder examined the vehicle and said that it was a simple job as he could do the welding to the mounting without dismantling anything, and I could have the vehicle in a short time. However, when I returned a little later, I found the gearbox and other parts lying on the floor of the garage!

The welder was not working on the vehicle, so I went to the foreman to ask him what was happening. He said, sharply, 'If you get this van tomorrow, you will be lucky.'

I then discovered that there had been trouble between the foreman and the welder. The welder had taken on the job without consulting the foreman who became very upset that he had been bypassed and made the welder dismantle parts which the welder felt was not necessary. I tried to point out to the foreman that we had to be in Johannesburg the next day to commence services, but in his anger he just ignored me.

I asked him if I could see the manager, but he refused to give me permission. Just then a door near where we were standing in the building opened and out stepped a neatly dressed gentleman. I presumed he was the manager so I approached him. When he confirmed that he was the manager I explained the position to him and how disappointed I was to find that the garage had done work in excess of what I had agreed, and that I would not be able to keep my appointment in Johannesburg. Putting a hand on my shoulder he said, 'My friend, you will have your vehicle tonight!'

He then went to the foreman and said, 'The welder must stay on the job tonight until that van is completely repaired.' We went out into the grounds of the garage, found seats and had some time to contemplate on what had happened and to wonder what the bill would be. As we estimated the number of hours that work was being done on the van, including over-time, and the fact that we did not know anyone in the city, we could not think of how the bill could be met. But we knew the

Lord and had proved that He never failed in time of need, so we prayed and rested in Him by faith that He would solve the problem!

Just before 9.00 pm the manager came to see us, and with 'fear and trembling' we waited to hear what we had to pay. He said, 'At this late hour our cashier has gone home, and he has locked the cash office. Please give me your address in Johannesburg and we will send on the account. Your van is now ready.'

How we praised the Lord as we collected our vehicle and started off on the journey south. We slept a short time in the van and reached Johannesburg the next day as originally planned.

When we arrived at the home of the minister who was arranging our appointments in South Africa, he was full of apologies and said, 'I was instructed to send you a cheque to cover your expenses on the way down, but I forgot to do so. Please forgive my neglect.' He then handed me a cheque which not only covered the cost of travel, but gave me enough money to pay for the repair account when it arrived. He did not know that because of his neglect, we had two fierce battles of faith, one for the money to continue the journey from Blantyre and the other when we thought that we would have to pay for the repairs the day of the breakdown.

But the Lord knew and He allowed these battles to take place to strengthen our faith and confidence in Him. The battles and the victories of faith did our souls good and filled our hearts with praise for and confidence in such a caring heavenly Father.

The meetings which took us to all four provinces of South Africa were mostly arranged for Christians. The weeks we spent there were very happy ones as we had fellowship with many devoted servants of the Lord, seeking light from His Word on the subject of revival and the importance of being 'sanctified,

meet for the Master's use, and prepared for every good work'
(2 Timothy 2:21).

The Vehicle in 'Hospital'

Before leaving the account of the above trip with its mechanical trouble and the Lord's provision, I will describe two other wonderful experiences we had as a result of vehicle trouble. One was in Tanzania, a few months earlier. One morning we found the battery was flat and although we pushed the van it would not start. We were many miles from any garage or source of help.

I found myself praying, 'Lord, I know that You can perform divine healing on the human body when it is your will. Would You please heal this battery until we get to a place where we can purchase a new one? We cannot carry on Your work with the battery in this condition!'

When we tried to start the vehicle again, the battery revived and we had no more trouble with it for three months until we reached a town where batteries were available. When we entered the town the battery 'died' and we had to buy a new one. Some may question if that was really a miracle and if it was right to ask the Lord to heal a battery. It certainly was a miracle as far as we were concerned, but one that would not be required in a country where help is available.

The other problem took place around the time of the political troubles in Malawi. The van was giving us suspension trouble and we could not locate the cause. I felt that I needed the advice of the agents for the makers of the vehicle. Although their workshop was in Blantyre, 400 miles away from our base in Mzimba, I decided that I had to make the journey as the trouble might develop into something quite serious.

Isabel went with me part of the way and stayed with missionaries of the Zambesi Mission at Ntonda. A sad accident happened near the mission station at that time. A local farmer had been troubled with wild pigs getting into his maize fields and damaging the crops. He borrowed a shot gun from the missionary, and when he heard rustling and saw movement among the stalks of maize he fired into the area. It was not a wild pig, but a little girl who had wandered into the maize. She died instantly.

When the man found out what he had done, he dropped the gun and ran off as fast as he could, calling, 'I am going to the flag! I am going to the flag!' He ran to the government centre where the flag was flying. He knew that the relatives of the little girl would be very angry and he would be in danger of being beaten to death if they found him. I understand that he was held in the centre until a court case could be held.

What a wonderful picture of the Lord's provision in Canaan when He required 'cities of refuge' to be built for such an event. It also illustrates the 'City of Refuge' we find in Christ as our Saviour when we run to Him to be saved from the just punishment that is due to us for our sins and receive His grace – the cancellation of what we rightly deserve.

After leaving Isabel at Ntonda I continued on to Blantyre. As our funds were quite low at that time we were both praying that the repair bill would not be beyond our means!

On arrival at the garage, the vehicle was examined and the mechanic said it was a simple job and I was to call back to collect it in the afternoon. When I returned I was told that the trouble was more serious than had been thought and would require two more days of work! My first reaction was alarm – the cost of all those hours of work plus spares for which I would be charged – when the purse was nearly empty. But then I remembered that we were on His Majesty the Lord's service. It was my responsibility to trust Him to provide what I needed in His service. I must admit that I had to fight a temptation to question how He could do that in such a short time in a city where I was a stranger. It would need to be a miraculous way for the Lord to get sufficient money to me before I had to pay! But none came before I had to collect the van!

When I went to the garage, again it was with 'fear and trembling' inwardly. I asked the workshop foreman if my van was ready, and he said to my surprise, 'Yes, but the manager wants to see you.'

After I entered the manager's office, he presented me with a very large account for labour and spares! I suspect he was watching me intently and perhaps noticed some concern on my face because he quickly added, 'Mr Selfridge, all you have to do is to sign that the work has been done. We have had a letter from the Rootes Group in England who manufactured the vehicle, stating that if you called with us we should check your vehicle thoroughly, do any repairs and send the account and report to them. They were interested to know how the vehicle was standing up to the African roads and weather.' It was one of the first of that model to come off the assembly line and to be tried on such roads and conditions.

After thanking him for all the help that he and his workmen had given, I walked out of his office praising the Lord and feeling as if I was walking on air. I had never thought that the manufacturers would get involved in helping to answer our prayer! The Lord likes to surprise us, so that we do not tie Him down to working in ruts.

But the Lord had another surprise for me, He decided to do 'exceeding abundantly above all that we ask or think' (Ephesians 3:20). Before I left Mzimba to go to Blantyre, a missionary in the north asked me to take a small parcel to a missionary nurse who was working in the mission hospital in Blantyre. When I had delivered the parcel and was about to drive away, she threw an envelope into the van and said, 'I did not know what to do with this tithe money yesterday, but I know what to do with it today!'

Later, when I opened the envelope I found that it contained

£50 which was a lot of money in those days – and the money had come from a missionary whose salary was very modest. When I arrived back at the mission station where I had left Isabel, her first question was, 'Did you have enough money to pay the bill?' She had been praying and trusting while I was away!

I replied, 'I have returned with more money than I had when I left'. Then I had the thrill of narrating how the repairs were paid by the manufacturers. I showed her the envelope with the £50 and told how it was thrown into the van and by whom. We praised the Lord together for His wonderful provision, especially for the miraculous way in which the manufacturers had been able to contact the garage where we had the largest bill for the van we had had up to that time.

13

Activities at the Base

Invitations continued to come in for special evangelistic services and conferences for Christians. Also people were coming to the base with their spiritual problems and seeking to find the way of salvation. Missionaries from isolated stations were also arriving for fellowship.

Not long after our house was finished, I was standing on the veranda and saw a lorry stopping. A well dressed young African man jumped off the lorry and came running over to me. He told me that he was a civil servant, working in the capital which was 400 miles away. As a member of the chief's clan he was returning from a meeting with other members. He wanted to talk to me, but the lorry driver said he would only wait five minutes.

He then quickly informed me that he knew Edward the headmaster whose conversion I have mentioned in the chapter on revival in the church. He said he had seen a great change in Edward's life and he asked me, 'Can such a change happen to anyone or is it just for those who are going into the ministry?' He had heard that Edward was leaving his teaching post and going into theological training.

I explained as best I could, in the few minutes at my disposal, that the wonderful experience of the new birth is for all who will accept Jesus as Saviour and Lord of their lives. As the lorry was ready to leave I suggested that we correspond. He gave me his name and address, and rushed back to the lorry. We will call him Matthew. We began to correspond by letter. He admitted that although he was a church member he had been guilty of many things which were displeasing to the Lord. I continued to share God's plan of salvation with him, explaining Christ's atonement for sin on the cross and God's willingness to forgive and never remember our sins against us again when we accept Jesus as our Saviour.

After a few weeks I received a wonderful letter from him.

'I was awake at 3.30 am and as I lay in bed, my sins seemed to be passing before me in a queue and all I could do was to cry to Jesus for forgiveness. Suddenly, as I trusted Jesus to accept me, I had the assurance that he had heard my prayer and that I was forgiven. I got out of bed, feeling that I must share my joy of forgiveness with others. So I dressed and went round the homes of my friends, knocking them up, and inviting them to my house, saying that I had an important announcement to make. My house was full of my friends just after 4.00 am and I shared my experience with them.'

He went on to tell me that the next morning when he went to the office, he felt such joy that he put his arm around the neck of the white man who was his boss, and said, 'I am your brother if you love the Lord Jesus.'

The boss was an unbeliever and responded by phoning the mental hospital and asking to have the man admitted for observation! An ambulance arrived and he was detained in the hospital. Eleven days later, he was sent back to the office by the psychiatrist, with a note for his supervisor. The note stated, 'All I can find wrong with this man is a sore finger.'

The boss sat down with Matthew and questioned him about what had happened that morning resulting in his excitement about Jesus. Matthew took his Bible and pointed out the verses which explained the new birth. His supervisor asked Matthew if he could take the 'book' home to show the verses to his wife, and he was given the use of the Bible.

Some weeks later, Matthew wrote to me and told me a dream. He dreamed that he had a very bad disease. The disease was the love of money! He asked if I thought he should apply to enter the ministry of the church, as he would then have a much smaller salary and less temptation to love money.

I wrote telling him that would be the wrong motive for entering the ministry. He must have a clear call that the Lord wanted him to preach the gospel. After a short time I got a reply, in which he wrote, 'I was in church on Sunday and the minister announced that the congregation was no longer able to support the full-time lay evangelist who helped the minister, so he was being made redundant. I felt God was speaking to me, showing me that I could use my extra money to allow the evangelist to continue his work for the congregation. At the end of the service, I went to the minister and talked over the situation with him. I found that with my salary, as a top civil servant, I would be able to give enough each month to support the evangelist. I promised the minister that I would take the responsibility to do that while I was employed in government service.'

The day did come when Matthew felt a call to the ministry. He applied to his own denomination, the Church of Central Africa Presbytery, and was accepted for theological training. That was in the 1960s and he has had over thirty years of fruitful ministry in different congregations and positions in the departments of the denomination. At the time of writing, he has recently retired as a parish minister and is the travelling evangelism secretary in the north of Malawi for the Evangelical Fellowship of Malawi.

One of the requests for services which we received at that time came from the Livingstonia Secondary School chaplain. He felt that a series of evangelistic services, with opportunities for counselling, would be very profitable from a spiritual standpoint for the hundreds of students who were enrolled there. We accepted his invitation and great interest was shown by the students. Many came for personal consultations about the subjects dealt with in the services. A number made decisions to give their lives to Christ, and it was felt by the staff that a new atmosphere of interest in spiritual things had developed in the school as prayer and Bible study groups were formed among the students. We gave God the praise and glory for His blessing on the young people who would be going out to important positions in the nation, with opportunities to serve Him.

Husband and Wife Reconciled

A young man who worked on the mission station, but not in the school, came to share his heartbreaking story. He had discovered his wife in the act of adultery, and felt that he could never forgive her although she said she was sorry and asked to be forgiven.

I suggested that he bring his wife along so that we could talk the matter over together, which he did. She assured us with tears that she was really sorry for what had happened. A friend of her husband had tempted her, but she said she had learned her lesson and that she would never be involved in that way again. I asked her husband why he was not willing to forgive her. He claimed that although she said she was sorry, it was only because he had found her out; she could not do anything else but say she was sorry, so he did not believe that it was genuine sorrow or repentance.

We then discussed Jesus' statement in the prayer which He taught, 'Forgive us our debts, as we forgive our debtors', and also His warning, 'If ye forgive not men their trespasses, neither will your Father forgive your trespasses' (Matthew 6:12, 15). At that stage in our discussion I suggested that I should leave them alone for fifteen minutes so that the wife could explain to her husband the depth of her sorrow. When I returned they were both smiling and assured me that there was forgiveness and reconciliation.

The three of us then knelt and they repeated their marriage vows to one another before the Lord. After prayer they left united in Jesus. Twenty years later I was informed by a missionary that they were still living a happy married life together.

However, such a result did not turn out that way in the life of a married couple who lived in another part of Africa where I had been asked to have services. I will share the details here, as their story contrasts radically with the above account.

The husband in this case remained behind for counselling after an evangelistic service. He prayed and asked forgiveness for many sinful things he had done, including unfaithfulness to his wife. One of those who came for spiritual help the next night was a woman who was deeply convicted for adultery. In conversation with her, I discovered that she was the wife of the man who had prayed the previous night. She too asked the Lord for forgiveness and expressed faith in Christ's atonement for her sins.

On the morning of the third day, the wife came back to see me, with her face very badly bruised and reporting bruises on many parts of her body. I asked her what had happened. She said, 'When I went home last night, knowing that Jesus had forgiven me, I felt that I should open up to my husband about my unfaithfulness and ask for his forgiveness. He became very, very angry and beat me violently! That is why I am in this condition.' I discovered that he had not told her about his past life!

I asked if her husband was at home. She said he was, so I suggested that we both go back to their house. When we arrived I asked him why he had caused such injuries to his wife. He said, 'She has been involved with other men, and has not been faithful to me. I am not going to put up with such conduct in my wife, so I felt that she needed a good beating, which I have given her.'

I then challenged him in front of his wife, 'The previous

night you told me about the kind of life you have been living and how unfaithful you have been to your wife. You prayed and told Jesus you were sorry for that sinful way of living and asked Him to forgive you. You said that you were trusting Him to forgive and change you so that you could live the Christian life. Now after asking Jesus to forgive you, when your wife comes and asks you to forgive her, you beat her severely.'

'It is different with a wife,' he replied, and became very angry with me for pointing out in front of his wife the kind of life he had been living. But as I felt his insincerity had to be confronted, I told him, 'Jesus said, "If you forgive not men their trespasses, neither will your heavenly Father forgive your trespasses", so if you are unwilling to forgive your wife, according to these words, you cannot expect to be forgiven by God.'

'I will never forgive her,' he adamantly replied. I prayed for them both before I left, asking that the Lord would give the wife the grace to live the true Christian life in front of her unforgiving husband. I asked the Lord for His Holy Spirit to continue to convict the husband so that he would see the seriousness of his mistaken attitude and repent. I was sorry to have to leave them in that sad state, but the incident took place in an area where I have never had the opportunity to minister again and I was not able to find out how the Lord answered prayer for the couple.

14

Events of the 1960s

The 1960s were very eventful years for us as missionaries and as a family. Harry Scott who had been with us in Mzimba for some months had the joy of welcoming from Ireland the young woman to whom he was engaged, Evelyn, who had the same surname. So we had a wedding in the local village, with a 'feast' for the local congregation.

After almost eight years of marriage and the assurance of doctors that Isabel would never be able to have a baby, our doctor gave her the exciting news in October, 1960 that she was three months pregnant! That caused great rejoicing and praise to God.

We had just come back from a trip to Zimbabwe where we had gone to collect the family of Isabel's nephew, Billy Dalby. I mentioned in a previous chapter that because of the rebellion in Zaire they had to escape to an airport during the night. They were taken to Salisbury (now Harare in Zimbabwe). When they arrived there they sent us a telegram to inform us of the situation.

As the telegram ended with the words 'Kill Anna', we thought that his wife Anna had been killed and asked the post office to check the message. We were informed that it should have read 'Bill Anna' which were both their names. We decided to go the 800 miles to collect them and sent a telegram which also had a wrong spelling when it arrived! The message should have read, 'Arriving Thursday. Prepared to bring you here. Selfridges.' The telegram had to be sent through the Red Cross as the refugees were being looked after by their staff. When the telegram arrived at the Red Cross office, a young woman read the message over the phone to Billy. She read, 'Arriving Thursday. Prepared to bring you here. Sausages.'

Billy said, 'We do not need sausages, we are being well fed!' 'Oh', the lady's voice continued, 'Sausages is the name of the senders!'

It was on our way back to Malawi with the family in a little Volkswagen Beetle car that Isabel did not feel very well, but was glad when the doctor told her the reason later!

The evangelism programme in Malawi continued to interest the leaders of the United Church of Zambia. The large area of the Copperbelt with its many mines employed thousands of men from different parts of Zambia as well as Malawi and Zaire. These men lived either in hostels or in large townships with their families and many of them were not being reached by the churches.

The United Church of Zambia was formed by the churches of a number of different societies to avoid overlapping in their outreach and care of the Christians. Missionaries from the Church of Scotland, London Missionary Society, Methodist, United Church of Canada and the Paris Evangelical Mission worked in the United Church which had become indigenous, with control in the hands of local African leaders.

The Rev. Bill Hincks was still the convener of the evangelism committee of the church, and through his committee we were invited to go back to Zambia for a period of three months in 1961 to train elders and other local lay leaders. We were offered the use of an empty mission house in the town of Ndolo.

In the meantime some complications had arisen with Isabel's pregnancy. The doctor was unhappy about her condition. We too were concerned, but Isabel felt she had received a promise from the Lord not to worry. The text she read in her daily reading stated, 'For I know the thoughts that I think toward you, saith the Lord, thoughts of peace, and not of evil, to give you an expected end' (Jeremiah 29:11). She believed that 'an expected end' was a promise from the Lord that she would have the baby she was expecting.

The doctor ordered her to bed for a period. In fact it was during that period that we had the riot in the church and were threatened with death. The doctor's orders meant that Isabel could not go with us that day. We were so glad afterwards that she was not there as she could have lost the baby. Eventually the doctor said he was unwilling to take responsibility for her after the seventh month and that she must be under the care of an obstetrician. The baby was due in April, so we arranged to go to Zambia in January as Isabel had been referred to a doctor there. We gratefully accepted the offer of the house and I agreed to be available for the elder training programme from February to May.

I drove over by car and Isabel went by air, having to change planes twice. A small plane which was able to land in an airfield in our village took her the first 200 miles. Unfortunately, the conditions for flying were not good for a small plane, but the pilot decided to take the trip to the other airport where she had to change planes. Isabel and another pregnant patient were the only passengers. As the plane had no windscreen wiper the pilot flew low, with his head out the window. He was taking his bearings from the ground!

Soon after we arrived it was time for me to start the training courses. There was a good response from the elders. We targeted one of the towns each week. The local elders in that town met for a training session after work each afternoon. On Saturdays we went to the markets and beer-gardens for large open-air services. On Sundays we joined in local churches for worship and Bible teaching in the morning and evangelistic services in the afternoon. As the elders witnessed for Christ during the months we were there, we had the joy of seeing many of the miners and their families turning to the Lord Jesus for salvation.

We had interesting experiences with hecklers, especially with some who were drunk, when we had open-air meetings near beer-gardens. These were large open spaces equipped with tables and chairs, and the locally brewed beer from maize was served from a central point. We did not attempt to have the service in the garden, but just outside the fence so that anyone who wished could come out and listen. I remember one amusing although serious incident.

A very drunk man pushed his way into the middle of the open-air crowd which was listening to the speaker. He stood in the middle and began to imitate the one who was witnessing. A drunk woman who was in the crowd, pushed her way into the centre and gave him a scolding. Then closing her fist, she struck him such a blow on the jaw that he fell to the ground. She then folded her arms and stood to hear what the speaker was saying. The man gradually got to his feet and staggered off into the crowd, giving no more trouble. The thought that came into my mind as I watched the effect was, 'The devil casting out devils!'

As the time drew near for 'the expected end' the obstetrician thought that Isabel would need a Caesarean Section.[1] But Isabel delivered the baby naturally on Sunday the 9th of April, 1961 – a girl, and we had the name Ruth ready if the Lord gave us a girl. I will take space in another chapter to explain the great joy she brought into our lives as she grew up with us, and also details of her childhood, schooling, and eventual nurse's training.

Myra Leslie Arrives to help in the Work
While we were still on the Copperbelt after Ruth's birth, we had the joy of welcoming a young woman from Shetland, Myra Leslie, who felt a call from the Lord to come and help us in the

1. Readers may remember that I wrote earlier about Festo Kivengere and William Nagenda of Uganda. I told of their visit to Isabel in hospital, and their prayer for her at an important time in her pregnancy. Their visit took place at the beginning of April.

work we were doing. She came by air from Britain to Ndolo Airport, so that she could travel back with us from Zambia to Malawi. Myra had been a close friend to Isabel for some years. They met in 1951 at evangelistic meetings being held near her home in Shetland. Isabel was there as part of the team conducting the evangelistic outreach. While Myra and Isabel were out walking together one day and discussing God's way of salvation, Myra decided to invite Jesus into her life as her Saviour and Lord.

Soon after her conversion, she felt the call to offer herself for full time missionary service. After training, she applied to come out to Mzimba where we were based. Her application was accepted and her arrival coincided with our stay in Zambia. We four, Myra, Isabel, Ruth and I, travelled back by road to Malawi, a journey of three days.

With Myra's arrival in Mzimba, our staffing was changed. Harry and Evelyn Scott were transferred to the Copperbelt to follow up the elders' training programme and to organize Christian literature distribution in the mining towns. With the recommendation of the churches, he appointed elders as 'book stewards', supplying them with stock, and travelling around at regular intervals to collect the money from the sales and renewing their stock.

Myra took over the office work at Mzimba as well as travelling out to centres of population with literature. She also helped Isabel in the work among the local women and relieved us from time to time as 'babysitter'. Above all she was a wonderful companion for Isabel who had often felt lonely and isolated when I was away on campaigns.

15

Medicine and Evangelism

Travelling so often in remote areas we were hundreds of miles from a doctor and dentist. When we would arrive in a village, before any services could start many came to us begging for help with their medical and dental problems. Isabel was a nurse and I had some medical training and a few old dental forceps, so we did what we could to relieve pain, treat malaria, bilharzia, dysentery and other complaints. But dentistry was a problem. For me to extract teeth, having had little instruction and being unable to inject anaesthetic, was a painful operation for the patient.

A dentist in Glasgow had given me the forceps and a few ideas on how to use them. When we first arrived in Malawi, there were four dentists for 5,000,000 people and around thirty doctors! During our stay in Malawi the population grew to 10,000,000!

We were informed that the Missionary School of Medicine in London offered a course in dentistry and other medical courses to missionaries who were based far from doctors and dentists. I decided to apply and was accepted for a special crash course, offered to me on my next home leave which commenced later in 1961. On finishing the course I was given a certificate in dentistry, eye diseases and homoeopathic medicine. It was not a full qualifying course in these subjects, of course, and was only for countries where fully trained persons were not available. On the basis of the training which I had received, the Malawi Government gave me permission to practise. As some people were living about 400 miles or more from a dentist, it meant that we were able to use anaesthetics, do fillings, provide dentures and medicines.

When we returned to Malawi after the course, word soon spread that teeth could be extracted painlessly and we were inundated with patients. Some days from just after 6.00 am people arrived holding their jaws. Often the patients continued until sunset! They came from as far away as 200 miles. It became necessary to build a special room in our garden as a clinic to attend to teeth, provide medicine and spectacles.

During the course at the MSM in London, the staff informed us of how we could buy equipment quite cheaply in certain shops which were selling off surplus military and air force equipment.

I was able to purchase a dental chair and drill which had been used by air force dentists as they travelled around the different camps during the war. The chair folded down into quite small space, but was capable of being unfolded into different angles and heights. That made it easier for us to take it with us into the villages where we were ministering. The dental drill had a treadle, like an old type of sewing machine, as we had no electricity. It was difficult for one to pedal and drill at the same time, as the movement of the foot made the hand shake! I always had to get someone to pedal as I drilled. Quite often it was Isabel, because local people who were not used to a treadle would allow it to go into reverse movement, causing the drill to turn in the opposite direction and so hinder the drill from cutting!

It was a problem to arrange appointments which made it difficult to organise our time. Few people had watches, clocks, calendars or diaries! They judged the time by the sun, so eventually we had to set certain hours when the clinic would be open, otherwise most of the day was taken up, as one after another arrived, leaving little time for spiritual activities.

Although we had the clinic in Mzimba, and I did a dental

clinic in the local hospital each week, we were also called on to help people in the villages when we were there for services. Sometimes when we went into a village where it had been announced ahead of time that we were coming, there would be a large queue waiting for medical or dental help. With such a situation we divided the patients. Isabel would attend to those needing medical help while I tried to deal with those who had toothache. I have known of as many as fifty waiting for extractions.

With such a large group, and not too much time at our disposal before the service was due to start, it was impossible to treat each patient as a dentist would do in a well equipped surgery in Britain. There an injection is given and about five or ten minutes are spent talking before the work on the tooth is started, knowing that the next patient has a set time to arrive. We gave about ten patients their injections and asked them to wait for the anaesthetic to take effect. Then they would be called back one by one for the extractions. Sometimes we found one of the ten would be missing and on enquiring what had happened would be told, 'Oh, that person decided that it was a very good injection that had been given, and because there was no more pain in the tooth, he (or she) decided to go home, and not bother getting the tooth extracted!' Of course, before the patient would reach home the pain would come back and it would be too late for a change of mind, as we too would be on our way home from the village by the time the patient could return.

A difficult wisdom tooth

As the government dentists were so far away from the north of Malawi, quite a number of missionaries came to us for treatment. One of them gave us great concern one Christmas eve. She was a nursing sister from Ekwendeni Mission Hospital, about seventy miles away, a missionary from the Presbyterian Church in Ireland. I knew her from the time she was a school girl as I used to visit her home when I was a student, and had the joy of introducing her mother to the Lord Jesus as her Saviour.

She arrived at our door, and said, 'Jack, I have a terrible toothache from one of my wisdom teeth. Would you please remove it?' As the tooth was impacted in the jaw bone, the local injection was ineffective, so she asked for a general anaesthetic.

I had an arrangement with the local government hospital that if anyone needed a general, it would be arranged for me in the operating theatre where the staff would be responsible to administer the anaesthetic. I rang the hospital and was given permission to take the patient there. The person responsible for the hospital was a clinical officer. Clinical officers were men who did not have the qualifications to take a university degree, but were given a special medical and surgical course to overcome the shortage of qualified doctors in Malawi. They were permitted to do almost everything that a qualified doctor could do.

The anaesthetist was a male nurse who had been given a course in anaesthetics. He had great difficulty in getting the syringe needle into a vein to administer Pentathol. However, when he finally succeeded, he gave the patient an overdose. She stopped breathing and began to turn blue. As Isabel prayed and I prepared to resuscitate her, the anaesthetist called out, 'Don't worry, that often happens here!'

We were very glad when breathing commenced again, although she remained in a very deep state of anaesthesia, which was to my advantage as it was a very difficult extraction. However, it took the sister about twenty-four hours to recover from the overdose instead of the usual five or ten minutes for an extraction. She had to remain with us over Christmas. Although it was the hot season of year in the tropics, Isabel had to keep her supplied with hot water bottles to overcome the shock her system had received. She had no Christmas dinner that year! It would have been very difficult for me to contact her mother in Ireland if the experience in the theatre had caused death.

The biggest coward who ever sat on the dental chair

The white man who was the area manager of the bus company stopped me in the village and said, 'I have been thinking of coming to see you. I am having toothache, but if I sit on your dental chair, I will be the biggest coward who ever sat on it!' I invited him to come up to the clinic and I would have a look at his tooth.

When he arrived and sat on the chair, he looked at me and said, 'The last time I was on a dentist's chair, the dentist took two-and-a-half hours to remove a tooth.' Although I knew that he was known to blaspheme, when he lost his temper, I said, 'Let me pray that the Lord will help me to remove your troublesome tooth.'

'Go ahead, Father, I also pray!' was his reply (he was a Roman Catholic). After prayer, I gave him an injection and was waiting for the jaw to become anaesthetized when he asked, 'Are you only giving me one injection? The dentist gave me twelve injections the last time and I still had severe pain!'

'If you feel pain when I commence the extraction, I will give more anaesthetic,' I assured him.

I later discovered that he had been a pilot in the Rhodesian Air Force and had crashed on one occasion, breaking his jaw. I came to the conclusion when I examined his mouth that the last extraction had involved a tooth from the area of the fracture and no doubt it had adhered to the bone during the healing process, hence the dentist's problem. I understand that the dentist had not been told about the fracture and so had the great difficulty with that particular tooth.

I had no problem in removing the tooth which was troubling him as it was from a different area of the jaw. He could not believe that it was extracted in a few seconds. He jumped off the chair, danced around the room and pressed some money into my hand. Then he said, 'I am having trouble with two more teeth, I think you should extract them while you are on the job!'

I looked at the teeth and thought it might be possible to save them as they were loose because of gum trouble. I suggested that he go to an American Mission Dental Clinic in Blantyre, the commercial capital of Malawi at that time. It was 400 miles away, but as he was manager of the buses travel was not a problem to him.

Some weeks later he came back and said, 'I have been to the dentist in Blantyre who confirmed that the teeth needed to be extracted.'

I asked him if the dentist had extracted them, and he replied, 'No way! I told him that he was not to extract them, as I had my own dentist in Mzimba and I left his surgery!' That surgery was the most modern and fully equipped dental clinic in Malawi, so I felt greatly embarrassed. He could not grasp the fact that it was not the original dentist's fault that he had such trouble. Perhaps he thought the prayer had brought success! He then asked me to extract them which I did without any trouble.

However, all patients do not take the same attitude to prayer. A woman, for whom a mission doctor prayed before administering the anaesthetic, told her friends when she returned home, 'Do you know what happened? The doctor did not know what to do with me. He had to pray!'

There was not much opportunity to do fillings in Africans' teeth. Most did not know that fillings were possibilities as there were so few dentists, so teeth were allowed to deteriorate until they were too far gone to fill. However, when extracting I would sometimes notice a tooth with a small cavity that could be saved. With the patient's permission I would fill it. Then I began to receive requests for 'cement' as the filling became known in the villages. Cement was the nearest they had seen to dental filling materials, but usually it was too late to save the tooth.

In earlier days, when tea and refined sugar had not been introduced to Central Africa, people chewed sugar cane. That had the double effect of providing the needed sugar and at the same time cleaning the teeth. The chewing also strengthened the enamel of the teeth. Although sugar cane is still chewed, when people began to drink tea and sweetened it with four spoonfuls of sugar on average for each cup, it was not long before teeth began to suffer. Toothpaste and tooth brushes are either not available or very expensive and so are beyond the reach of the majority. It was very sad to see, not only adults, but also children losing their teeth, when previously Africans were known for their strong and beautiful teeth.

Sometimes we had fun when extracting teeth from those who had some education, as that seemed to give them a greater fear of pain. Often after I had already got a grip of a tooth, patients would change their minds and decide not to have the tooth extracted, so they would try to pull my hand away. One day when I was doing a dental clinic in the hospital operating theatre, a man took my hand after I gripped the tooth, and when I refused to loosen my grip he jumped off the chair and took me around the operating table pulling my hand. I still maintained my grip, and eventually he pulled his own tooth!

On the other hand, old men and women who had suffered pain most of their lives, before modern medicine reached that part of Africa, would sit without showing any sign of nervousness, even when in many cases the tooth had to be extracted without anaesthetic because of abscesses.

In most cases the patients had to have their extracted teeth given back to them. That necessity seems to have arisen from an old fear that if anyone hated them and wanted to harm them, that person could get hold of their tooth, take it to a witch doctor and have the owner bewitched! That applied not just to teeth, but to anything from the body like nail clippings or hair.

Provision of dentures was also a new idea to people who lived in the outlying areas. We were able to help some who found lack of teeth a drawback in public speaking, like teaching and preaching. Although I filled the teeth of quite a number of missionaries, I was not too happy about providing them with dentures, as I felt they could make plans to have them fitted in their own country when on leave. But I did make one exception.

Myra Leslie developed severe dental trouble and most of her remaining teeth could not be saved. She begged me to extract them and arrange for dentures, and finally I agreed. It was too difficult for me to prepare a temporary set of dentures. The wax models had to be sent to a dental technician. That meant that Myra was without teeth for six months until her mouth had healed enough for her permanent set. She had a cousin who was a dentist in Singapore, so we sent the model to him and when the dentures arrived they fitted well.

An amusing incident happened when she first appeared with her new teeth! Her original teeth had protruded a little, but she did not want the dentures to do that. She had been without teeth for a time and when she and Isabel went to visit some homes, they met with a group of ladies who asked Isabel: 'Where did that other woman go who used to work with you?'

Isabel was puzzled. She could not think of who the other woman was! After a further discussion, she found out that they did not recognise Myra with her new teeth! So the conversation ended with much laughter and slapping each other's hands, which is a common way of celebrating in Africa when something amusing or very interesting takes place.

On the subject of dentures, one other event caused us to laugh. An Asian came wanting dentures. After they were fitted, he came a couple of times, complaining that they were hurting him. I tried to explain that it takes a little time for the mouth to settle down to dentures, as I tried to relieve some pressure points.

Then one day he came and handed me the dentures saying, 'Just sell them to someone else!'

A Christmas baby

Christmas Day is usually a very busy day in the life of a missionary. There are services and also many visitors come to ask for 'Kisimas boxie' (a gift), so we sometimes postponed our family celebrations to Boxing Day, hoping for a quieter day. But that did not always happen.

On a particular Christmas night, soon after we had been stationed in Mzimba, we had gone to bed early, feeling quite exhausted with the activities of the day. We were looking forward to Boxing Day, hoping for a time of relaxation. But at 5.00 am we were wakened by loud knocking on our bedroom window, and the voice of a man outside asking us to come quickly to his village. He said his wife was very ill, having been in labour for two days. I rushed out to take her to the hospital, but found that the baby had been born, so I returned to the house to take Isabel to help the mother. When we arrived at the hut, and Isabel had seen the mother, she asked to see the baby.

Women who had gathered in the hut with the patient, pointed to a bundle of cloth in a corner of the floor. When Isabel removed the covers she found the baby bleeding from both hands. On investigating, she discovered that the baby had been born with six fingers on each hand, and one of the older women in the village had chopped off the extra fingers! Just then the mother lapsed into convulsions, so we had to try to stop the bleeding and get mother and baby to hospital – three miles away.

When we arrived at the hospital we found that the doctor who was in charge at that time had gone for a Christmas break and the medical assistant could not be found. Leaving the mother in the care of a midwife, Isabel and I went into the theatre and tied up the little arteries in the severed fingers. There could have been a double reason for removing the extra fingers. One would be the superstition associated with witchcraft, and the other that as the baby was a girl it would lower the value of the dowry which the father would receive when she grew old enough to marry!

In the evening we went back to the hospital to see the condition of mother and baby and found it in darkness, apart from an odd candle here and there. On enquiring what was wrong, we were told that the person responsible for the fuel store had gone to celebrate Christmas at a beer-party and had not returned with the keys of the store. The hospital was lit with paraffin-burning lamps, as there was no electricity in the hospital.

Isabel found that the nurses were doing all they could for mother and baby. But she discovered another patient who had given birth to triplets that day and there was no provision for the feeding of the three babies in the dark. She rushed back to our house to get a feeding bottle and a small oil lamp.

The next day when the doctor arrived, he came to our house to apologize for the conditions we found in the hospital and to thank us for what we had done. Since returning to Britain and hearing people criticising the hospital services, our minds go back to the conditions of many patients in Africa where they are often lying two or three in a bed, and quite often there are others under the bed!

Eighty pairs of spectacles in one day

In the villages we found many people whose eyesight had deteriorated. We were especially concerned about ministers, teachers, church elders and woman's guild leaders who were no longer able to read the Scriptures. With the shortage of ordained ministers and pastors, the elders were responsible for much of the preaching and teaching of church classes. Leaders of the woman's guild were usually older members and many of them were experiencing difficulty with reading.

We had friends in Britain who collected and sent out old spectacles which people no longer needed. There was a lot of difficulty in using these as we did not know the strength of the lenses. Some were bifocal and others had two different lens. We found that after trying a number of different pairs of spectacles the person was confused and could not decide if a pair suited.

One day in July 1960 when Isabel and I were having a few days rest in a mountain cottage, a stranger drove up in a car and announced that he represented an organization called 'Missionary Optical Services'. He had been told that we were in the cottage. His organization in England received used spectacles, measured the power of the lenses and labelled them. The person in charge was a qualified chemist and optician. They repaired or fitted new frames to the lenses, making sure that both lens were the same strength, and discarded bifocals, as these had to be individually inserted into spectacles for each person by an optician.

The MOS sent out parcels of assorted spectacles free of charge to missionaries who requested them. Each pair of spectacles was labelled, giving the strength of the lenses. MOS suggested it was better to make a small charge for each pair, as it was known that something free was never appreciated and looked after like something one had bought. When an item was given free it was sometimes thought that it was given because it was of such little value that it could not be sold! Missionaries were asked to use their discretion and if a person was poor and unable to pay they could have the spectacles free. Any money from the charges went back to MOS to help to cover the postage on the parcels.

Although we had a portable eye-testing kit, it was difficult with such large numbers to always take time to use it to choose the correct labelled spectacles. We have had as many as eighty people waiting in a village for spectacles as well as others for tooth extractions! In situations like that, we would usually ask the person to read from a book which we would give upside down! If the person did not notice that the book was upside down, we knew that a strong pair of spectacles was needed! If it was observed that the book was the wrong way up, we tried to judge the strength that was needed by how long it took the person to discover that fact.

It made things much easier when we had spectacles with marked lenses. We could try weaker or stronger ones and find out which gave a clearer reading. But we had a major difficulty with some people, especially students, who thought that spectacles were the badges of education and they only wanted them for show! In an effort to deal with that problem we had frames with no lenses. If we suspected that someone did not need reading spectacles, we would try one or two with lenses and then unknown to the person use the frames which had none. If they were considered perfect, we would take them off, put our fingers through the frames and show that 'glasses' were not necessary. What a look of disappointment would then appear!

It gave us great joy to see the reaction of those who could read again for the first time in many months or years. They would dance around in their excitement and expression of thanks and Isabel would get hugs from the women! Sometimes after taking off the spectacles to have a look at them, they would get mixed up as to how they should be put on again. They would try to fit them upside down, hooking them under the ears instead of over the top. The labels which were on the lenses to show their strength were often kept by the people as decorations!

After giving spectacles we tried to provide some good gospel reading material to each person. Our intention was not only that the literature would help the readers, but often they liked to show that they could read again and would do so in a public place where a group soon gathered to listen!

16

Family Life

The arrival of our daughter Ruth in April 1961 resulted in a number of obvious changes in our lives and activities. While Ruth was a small baby, Isabel and I were no longer free to go together on long preaching safaris in our van.

The travelling and camping would have been too much for the baby, especially with many of the conditions that could arise. I have had to have a team of eight oxen pull the vehicle out of mud. Isabel and I have been stuck in a river and had to sleep in the van there all night until we were able to get a tractor to pull us out the next morning. Another evening, just as darkness was falling, we had to travel on a very muddy road with a steep hill. The van skidded so much we had to stop half way up the hill and remain there all night, hoping that no vehicle would come too fast in the opposite direction over the brow of the hill and be unable to stop! Also we were not able to live so freely in the village huts as there was a danger of ticks, which carry typhus, falling from thatch on to Ruth. Such difficulties meant that Isabel and Ruth stayed at the base when I was away on preaching tours.

However, Ruth brought great joy into our lives and a ray of sunshine into our home. It was a wonderful experience to see this little flower, which God had planted in His garden of the world, open up and blossom in such a fascinating way. The wonder increased as she began to take her own short steps when she was around eight months old.

The fact that Isabel now had a child drew the African women closer to her. Although their skins were different they had something in common – motherhood – and so could communicate on a common subject.

There were no other white children in our area and when Ruth was able to play outside she became quite an attraction for African children. Soon the space around our house became a scene of much activity! I built a small hut of mud and wattle twigs with a grass roof, a door and windows without glass. An African 'wendy' house! Ruth had many 'visitors' in her little 'home'. She was more fluent in the local language than we were as she learned it directly from the children. She also loved their food made from maize flour, called 'sima', much better than our meals in the house!

She also especially enjoyed the first rains in the first year she was able to be outside. She had not seen any rain for six months in the dry season and when it began to fall she wanted to go out and stand in it. Isabel dressed her in a long raincoat with a hood and she stood out in the shower shouting with glee. I could not confirm that she was 'singing in the rain'.

The day came when she began to notice that her skin was not the same shade as the children with whom she was playing. Being the only one with that colour of skin, one day when Isabel was bathing her, she asked me, 'Daddy, could you not paint me black?'

Isabel asked her, 'Why do you want to be painted black? Do you not want us to be your mummy and daddy any more?'

'No, I want you to be my mummy and daddy, but I want to be the same colour as the other children,' she assured us.

When I was leaving to go off alone for some meetings one day, she said to Isabel, 'The best thing about daddy going away is his coming back'.

Another time when I went into the bathroom, I found her standing beside the bath, holding a stick with a piece of string hanging from it into the bath water. I asked her, 'Ruth, what are you doing?'

'I am fishing, daddy,' she said, looking at me as much as to say, 'Can you not see that?'

I have often used that incident as an illustration when I preach on the subject of 'Fishing for men', pointing out that we cannot catch fish where there are no fish, just as Peter found out when he fished all night and caught none (Luke 5:5). As most of the people in the churches have already been 'caught' we must launch out from our churches into the places where non-Christians live.

An amusing incident happened one night when we were travelling in Tanzania. Ruth was still quite small and was sleeping in the back of the van. Suddenly in the lights of the vehicle we saw nine lions on the road. I drove up close to where they were and stopped. We called, 'Ruth, come and see what is on the road.' She came forward and looked out through the windscreen and then excitedly exclaimed, 'Daddy, take a fly-swatter and go out and kill one of them!' I did not take her advice.

We went back to Britain on leave in 1967 when Ruth was six years old. On the ship, as we approached Southampton, we found her crying on deck. We asked her what was wrong and she said, 'I don't know what to do with my hands, they are very cold'. That was her first experience of British weather and the first time she had needed gloves.

On the way she also asked, 'Is the Queen like Dr. Banda? We must go and see her!' She had met Dr. Banda and he had shaken hands with her and she wanted to do the same with the Queen! When we were in London, the Queen was meeting the King of Saudi Arabia at the Tate Gallery, so Ruth was able to see her in her horse-drawn coach.

That week when we were staying with friends in London, Ruth went to Sunday School, and a trip to the seaside was announced for the following Saturday. When Isabel was preparing her for the outing, and telling her she was going in a bus, she said, 'I am not going in a bus, the teacher said we would go in a coach.' She thought they would be pulled to the seaside by horses, in a coach like the one in which the Queen rode!

We spent some months of our leave in Ireland and Ruth went to my old school in Cullybackey for a few months by kind favour of the principal. She developed a lovely Cullybackey accent.

Ruth's Education

Planning her education caused problems. The nearest English-medium school open to white children was about 180 miles away. It was a government boarding school, but we could not think of parting with her for months at a time, when she would be only five or six years of age. Isabel began to explore methods of teaching Ruth at home.

The first method suggested to her was called 'Teach your Baby to Read', developed by an American, Dr. Dorman, who was a specialist in the field of medicine and education for brain-damaged children. In his research to help these children, he discovered that normal children had the ability to read at a much younger age than was usually thought. Using the methods which he had adopted, Isabel was able to succeed in getting Ruth to read simple sentences when she was around four years of age. From that time, she has continued to be an avid reader.

When Ruth was five years old, the question of her primary education had to be faced and prayed over to receive the guidance of the Lord. We felt it was an answer to prayer when another missionary mother told us of an organisation in England called 'Parents' National Education Union' (PNEU). It had been founded to help parents who were involved in overseas work in the diplomatic or other government service in countries where there was no English-medium school. Many missionary parents also took advantage of the scheme.

Isabel contacted their office in Britain and received a very warm response from the secretary, with details of how the primary education was arranged. Lessons and materials for each term would be sent out ahead of time and a test to which the child had to respond at the end of term. We felt that was an answer to prayer and although Isabel was a nurse and not a teacher, she was willing with the Lord's help to take the responsibility of teaching the course to Ruth.

We were very satisfied with the method. Ruth passed primary-one to primary-five before we were transferred to the city of Blantyre. She was able to take primary-six in St. Andrews Primary School there and also forms one and two in St. Andrews Secondary School. Unfortunately, St. Andrews Secondary School at that time only taught up to O level. There was no other school in Malawi teaching A level, in which white children were accepted.

Once again we were faced with a decision. We had to decide where Ruth would continue her secondary education, and we had the choice of two options:

1. We could end our work in Africa and go back to Britain as a family, where education would not be a problem, or
2. She could be sent back to Britain alone, and attend school there, either in boarding or with relatives.

We loved our work in Africa and as the Lord had called us to the work, we could not leave without very clear leadings from Him. And we had no assurance that was His will. As for the second option, there were obstacles arising from the financial angle. With no guaranteed allowance or salary, but trusting the Lord for the supply of our needs in His work, we felt that we should not commit ourselves to the fees that would be necessary to send her to a boarding school in Britain.

Relatives were willing to accommodate Ruth and she could have gone to a local school, but that meant that we would not see her for periods of perhaps three or four years at a time, because of the expense of flying her back during holidays. That was not an acceptable option either! So we went back to our heavenly Father for instructions.

We found that He was already preparing a third option. A missionary from South Africa, who was working in the Church of Central Africa Presbyterian in Malawi and with whom we had worked, knew about our problem. He wrote to the head-master of the Boarding School he had attended in Villiersdorp, South Africa pointing out our position, as the school was very interested in the children of missionaries. It was a bi-lingual-medium school – Afrikaans and English. On an average, eight missionaries' children from Malawi boarded at the school.

He had a very interesting reply from the principal, inform-ing him that if we were willing to send Ruth to the school, he was willing to arrange for her to have a bursary to cover her tuition and boarding! We were convinced that was an answer to our prayers. Our responsibility would be to provide uniform and air fare for holidays, which would be very much less than we would have had to pay from Britain.

However, another surprise awaited us when we took her to the school after driving her down for her first term. The acting headmaster told us to take her to the shop in the town which stocked the uniform and ask the manageress to provide Ruth with a full rigout of uniform at the school's expense! We figured that the cost involved was equivalent to over £100 in those days.

Ruth remained at the school for the rest of her secondary education and matriculated in 1979, and entered Nurse's Train-ing at the beginning of the following year. It was during her time at school, when she attended a church camp, that she made the decision to give her life to the Lord Jesus.

We were able to fly her back to Malawi twice a year during her time at school. One holiday in the middle of the year al-lowed her to be home for ten days. The other one, over Christ-mas and the New Year, gave her about four weeks because it was the Southern African summer and the end of the academic year. She had two other half-term holidays between these holidays, but because of expense we arranged for her to go to George and Vera Dunn, who had worked in Malawi, before retiring to South Africa. George was secretary of the Malawi Railways and he and Vera knew Ruth well.

Health

In Malawi, as a family we all had to take health precautions. Drinking water had to be boiled, as there was the danger of bilharzia, dysentery and cholera. There had to be protection as far as possible from the bites of mosquitoes to avoid malaria, so mosquito-gauze was fitted to windows and nets over beds. Naturally when Ruth was small we had to be especially careful. Bites of ticks living in grass could cause tick-typhus, and scorpions had a very painful sting! Ruth heard one fall on to her pillow one night and, not knowing what it was, she tried to push it off and was stung and suffered great pain for some time.

We had two anxious times with Ruth's health. On one occasion two doctors were very concerned about her heart. We were told not to allow her to climb trees or do any other strenuous activity until she could be taken the 400 miles south to Malawi's main hospital in Blantyre for a checkup.

At the hospital, the medical consultant pointed out that Malawi did not have a heart specialist. She said, 'Yesterday, we had one visit the hospital from South Africa, who would have been glad to see Ruth. But I can arrange an X-Ray and see if it reveals any abnormality.'

While Isabel, Ruth and the doctor went off to the X-ray department I sat in the waiting room. After a short time I was joined by another man. When the three returned from the X-Ray department, the doctor was surprised to see the person beside me. He rose and apologised to her for leaving his camera in the hospital the day before.

The visitor was the specialist! The doctor told him about Ruth and how glad she was that he had returned because of the lack of a cardiologist in Malawi.

He gave Ruth a thorough examination and then told Isabel, 'You do not need to worry about your girl. A nerve is causing the irregular beat, but the heart is perfectly healthy. You do not need to restrict Ruth in any way, she will grow out of the problem!'

What a wonderful relief not having to restrict her. She was free to play with other children again. Our source of joy and praise was not only for the good news about Ruth's condition, but also the wonderful way in which the specialist had returned so unexpectedly to the hospital, just at the time when Ruth was there. We felt that the Lord had performed a miracle. The specialist could have remembered the camera the previous day, or he could have returned for it either before we arrived at the hospital or after we had gone! God's timing was perfect. Just at the time when Ruth needed specialist attention, the Lord brought a cardiologist 2,000 miles. Praise was given to the Lord, it was His doing.

The second time of concern was when Ruth had chickenpox and a very severe attack of malaria at the same time. The nearest doctor was seventy miles away. We had the drug for malaria, but did not feel that we should give the injection to our own child without a doctor's permission. We prayed that the Lord would guide us in what we should do. The answer came again in an unexpected way! We were told that a doctor on holiday was spending the weekend in the government rest house in the village. We thanked the Lord, and I went to the rest house where I discovered that the doctor was the medical officer of health for Malawi!

I explained the situation to his wife and asked if her husband could please go immediately and see Ruth. The wife refused to ask him. She said, 'My husband is on holiday and will not get involved in any medical work in the village.'

I pled with her, explaining that there was no doctor within seventy miles and our daughter was very, very ill with a high temperature. She was adamant that her husband was resting during the weekend and that he was not available.

I refused to go away! I felt that Ruth's life was hanging in the balance. Something had to be done soon and inside the rest house was a man I felt held a key to her recovery. I prayed inwardly to the Lord and talked outwardly to the woman until at last she began to show signs of yielding to my pleading and said she would ask her husband.

When he appeared, I knew her reason for protecting him – he was drunk! Being away on holiday and in a village where he was not known, he had decided to have a weekend 'out of this world'! After some persuasion he eventually agreed to go with me. Staggering around Ruth's bed and paying most of his attention to her chickenpox, he refused to admit that she had malaria and would not give permission for her to have the injection. Isabel, as a nurse, tried to convince him because of Ruth's rigors and temperature, but he decided to leave without giving the necessary permission.

However, just as he was about to go out the door, he went back to the bed, examined her spleen and admitted, 'The spleen is swollen, she definitely has malaria, and should have an injection of Chloroquine.' Ruth got the injection and began to recover.

Again we felt that the Lord had worked things out in a miraculous way for Ruth. A doctor arrived in Mzimba that very weekend when she was so ill; his wife yielded and agreed to her drunken husband making the visit; and he visited Ruth and gave the necessary permission to inject. 'God works in a mysterious way His wonders to perform.' Our hearts were filled again with praise and thanks to Him.

17

Evangelism by the Church

When a church is revived, the result is *outreach evangelism* by its members. After people come to Christ and experience new life in Him, their longing and desire is to introduce others to Him. That is clearly illustrated in the New Testament. When Andrew met Jesus, he went and found his brother Simon and brought him to Jesus (John 1:40-42). In the same chapter John reports that after Jesus asked Philip to follow Him, he was concerned about Nathanael and invited him to 'come and see' Jesus. Then in chapter four, John describes how the Samaritan woman, as soon as she found Jesus and received the 'Water of Life', rushed off to her town and called people to 'Come, see a man who told me all things that ever I did, is not this the Christ?' We read that 'many of the Samaritans believed on Him for the saying of the woman'.

The revival which took place on the day of Pentecost when the Holy Spirit was poured out on the young church resulted in the Christians going out immediately on to the streets of Jerusalem and declaring that Jesus was the promised Messiah and Saviour.

It was not surprising then after times of reviving in Malawi that the evangelical missions and churches felt that there was a great need to reach out to the non-Christians with the good news of salvation. Also there was great concern because liberal theology was being introduced into Malawi by representatives of the World Council of Churches and scholarships were being arranged by them for Malawian ministers to go overseas to study at theologically liberal colleges.

Often representatives of the evangelical missions and denominations met to pray and discuss the situation. They decided to affiliate with the 'Association of Evangelicals of Africa and Madagascar', an organization which had its headquarters in Nairobi, Kenya. The Malawi branch became known as the 'Evangelical Fellowship of Malawi'.

I was asked to be the speaker in 1962 at a 'Keswick' type convention launched by the Fellowship, and was also appointed convener of the Evangelism Committee which was formed by the Fellowship. It was felt that the most effective way to counteract liberal theology was aggressive evangelism, where the lives of men and women were transformed by the Holy Spirit.

The evangelism programme was based on a theory suggested by a Presbyterian missionary in Latin America, a Rev. Strachan. He was very troubled by the fact that false cults like the Jehovah Witnesses, the Mormons and others were so successful in deceiving people and drawing them into their organizations. Many of those being attracted were from the established churches and missions. He became so concerned that he took two weeks local leave and shut himself away in a mountain rest house to pray and seek the Lord for an answer to the Satanic success of false cults. As a result of his time of waiting on God, he felt the answer given to him was this theory: 'The growth of any movement is in direct proportion to the success of that movement in mobilising its total membership in the constant propagation of its beliefs.'

I understand that Jehovah Witnesses are expected to spend at least fifteen hours each week propagating their beliefs! That is why we find them so often at our doors and on the street with their literature.

Some of the evangelical churches and missions in Latin America took Strachan's theorem seriously and launched a programme called 'Evangelism in Depth', where each Church member was expected to be a witness for Christ. An African pastor and a missionary in Nigeria went to South America to study the programme and returned with the desire to introduce the theory in Africa. However, they felt that the word 'evangelism' would turn off the Moslems from being interested, so the name they suggested was *New Life for All*.

The Evangelical Fellowship of Malawi invited the pastor and missionary to come to Malawi and explain how the theory worked out in practice. The Fellowship felt that it could be adapted for Christians in Malawi.

Now life for all
Here is a brief description of how the suggested programme was explained by these men.

The first step was for the minister or pastor to meet for discussion with the leaders of the organizations in his congregation – that is his session or council, woman's guild or group, Sunday school, youth groups, etc. The object of the discussions was to find the most effective way to mobilise the members of their organizations and through them the whole congregation. It was strongly stressed that each individual church member should seek to be a witness for Christ – at home, at work, travelling, shopping, visiting etc. Also leaders were responsible for devising methods to use in outreach in the parish or district, such as house-to-house visiting, open-airs and literature distribution.

The second step was for the church leaders, in sermons, visits and activities of their different organizations, to inspire their members to see from Scripture the importance of getting involved in witness. A series of twelve Bible Studies had been prepared, as it was important that the activities of the programme should be Bible-based. In addition, emphasis was laid on the importance of each witness being empowered by the Holy Spirit. It was suggested that each week for three months one of the twelve Bible Studies should be taught in small classes before outreach activities were organized.

The members of the Evangelical Fellowship were very interested in the ideas which the visitors from Nigeria presented, but felt the need of finding out the reaction of local church leaders. In 1969 a special retreat was held, bringing together representatives from almost all the Protestant missions and churches, not just those who were members of the Evangelical Fellowship. A few were not willing to co-operate, mostly because of liberal theological views of missionaries with whom they were involved. A large majority of those attending welcomed the opportunity to get help in enlisting, encouraging and instructing their members in the work of personal witness and evangelism. It was decided at the retreat to ask the evangelism committee to set things in motion to organize the programme.

A very unexpected development arose! The Evangelical Fellowship asked me to consider giving two years full-time as Organizing Secretary of the programme to get it off the ground, or should I say, out of the churches and into the community. It was not to be a one-off event, but the churches and missions were to use it in a continuous yearly cycle and they felt the need of a full-time organizer.

Organizing Secretary

It was a very big decision for us to make! If accepted, it would mean moving 400 miles south to Blantyre, the commercial capital of Malawi, as the majority of the population was in the southern region of the country, and the committee felt that it would be best to have the 'New Life for All' office there. We were too isolated in the north.

The position would be an honorary one, with no remuneration, and we would be responsible for our own accommodation. The committee knew that all our work up to that time was on a faith basis, looking to the Lord alone for our needs. As the Fellowship had no funds to spend on the programme, the committee thought we would have extra faith for the launching of the joint evangelistic project!

After much prayer and seeking the Lord's will, I thought that it was a call from God as the need was great, but Isabel had a much more difficult time coming to the same conclusion. I felt very sorry that she was faced with such a decision. Our house in Mzimba was the first 'home' in which we had lived together. The twelve years we had spent there meant much to Isabel after all our years of travelling. It was where Ruth had entered our lives and we had many spiritual children in the area, as well as many friends.

What made matters worse was that we had no idea where we would be living in Blantyre. Extra funds would be needed for rent as we were only promised free accommodation for six months in a house which was empty for that period. We did not want to sell our house at Mzimba as we had provided Myra Leslie with a flat in the grounds and it was her 'home' in Malawi. The appointment was to be for only two years so we expected to return to Mzimba after that time. Up to the last night before we were due to leave Mzimba, Isabel did not have peace about the move and that evening she was away alone in tears, pleading with the Lord to make it clear if it was His will for us to go. If it was His will, she wanted the assurance that He would supply the grace and strength to accept it willingly. She came away from her time with the Lord that night, assured that it was the Lord's will for us to go to Blantyre and that He would look after us. We moved at the beginning of 1970.

It was not easy to move away from the house which the Lord had given us the privilege of using all those years in Mzimba. They were very happy years as the Lord's work opened up for us. We had the privilege of using it as a base from where we travelled all over Malawi and to other countries to have evangelistic meetings, speak at conferences for missionaries and church leaders, and conduct training courses for lay people.

Over that period the Lord provided help for us in a wonderful way. Harry Scott, later joined by Evelyn, did a wonderful work with preaching and literature distribution in Malawi before being transferred to Zambia in 1962. Myra was the one who was with us for the longest period and also followed us to Blantyre later. She took over the literature distribution and helped in services after Harry and Evelyn went to Zambia. She also looked after Ruth when Isabel and I were both away. We did wonder at one time if we were going to lose her as she received a marriage proposal from a well-to-do South African farmer, but she was convinced that it was not the Lord's will for her life.

The next longest helper we had was Jean Wright, a teacher from London. She joined Myra and shared her flat, as well as the work she was doing, during most of the sixties.

My brother James arrived in 1968, hoping to marry Jean and also to get involved in our work, but there were very strict immigration laws in the country at that time and he was refused a work permit. When I went to see the Immigration officer who was a white official, he told me, 'Because of the regulations of the new government since independence, it is as easy to get a permit for a new missionary who wants to do evangelistic work as it is to find a snowball in hell!'

The Reformed Church in Zambia needed a general handyman/mechanic and James had taken courses in these subjects. When the Reformed Church heard that he was not accepted for work in Malawi they asked for his help. He went over to Zambia and it was not long until Jean followed him and they were married there. Later, James became the youth organizer for the Church and he and Jean worked for ten years in that position until they went to fill an appointment in Cape Town.

We had three others who helped us at different times for shorter periods. My sister Elizabeth, who had been a Faith Mission Pilgrim, was with us for one year, and Trudy Harvey from

Scotland also spent a year. We also had Judy Hopley from South Africa who had studied with Jean Wright in Emmanuel Bible College, Birkenhead.

No Fixed Abode!

During our first fourteen months in Blantyre, we were in six different houses, using homes of people who were on holiday or away for some other reasons. We had a very frightening experience with Ruth in one of these houses. She had placed something in a fridge and just after closing the door, the fridge was struck by lightning. A large ball of fire appeared on its top. We were very thankful to the Lord for His wonderful protection on her young life.

As the work of 'New Life for All' developed, we were gradually drawn to the conclusion that the Lord was showing us that it would be more effective for us to work out from Blantyre in future, rather than go back to Mzimba again after two years. With that in mind we began to explore the idea of selling the house in Mzimba and purchasing one in Blantyre to avoid continually changing from one house to another. We contacted the government housing department to ask if they would be interested in buying the Mzimba house. They offered us £4,500 although it had only cost us £1,200 to build. House prices had gone up after independence. We accepted the offer and began to look for a house in Blantyre.

When we found one that seemed suitable, the price asked was over £7,000. Houses were more expensive in the city and we had no other funds with which to bridge the gap. We felt the house would be ideal for us. Isabel had discovered it and fell in love with it right away. It is very important that the lady of the house feels that a house is suitable for a 'home'! Also it had a section which could be converted into an apartment for Myra as she also had to move to Blantyre when the house in Mzimba was sold. We prayed that if it was the Lord's will for us to buy the house, He would confirm it by providing the extra money. Then an unusual thing happened – we felt the Lord was asking us to give away some of the money we had received from the sale of the Mzimba house.

Financial sowing

The Lord brought to our minds a missionary and his wife who were also living by faith and trusting the Lord to provide for their needs. He seemed to impress on us that we should send the couple £400. At first, we felt we must be mistaken. We were praying that we would receive money, not for an opportunity to give some away! But as we meditated on the position, we were reminded of Paul's teaching on sowing and reaping: 'Whoever sows sparingly, will also reap sparingly, and whoever sows generously, will also reap generously' (2 Corinthians 9:6, NIV).

We also thought of Jesus' teaching on giving: 'Give, and it shall be given unto you; good measure, pressed down, and shaken together, and running over, shall men give into your bosom' (Luke 6:38).

Of course it would be wrong to give so as to receive good measure back for selfish purposes. God gives back for increased sowing! He wants the reaping to be used to further His work. We knew that it was the Lord reminding us that if a farmer keeps all his seed in the barn in springtime to use for food and feels that he could not spare any of it for sowing, he would eventually have none for food!

We accepted that it was the Lord's will for us to 'sow' some of the money we had received from the sale of the house. We wrote a letter to the missionary, who worked in another country, telling him about the money and asking him how he wanted it to be sent. We posted the letter and collected our mail from our personal box at the other end of the Post Office. When we opened one of our letters, we found it came from a retired business man in England, and it stated: 'I have £2,500 I would like to send you as a gift for your work, please let me know how you would like it to be sent.'

What a thrill we had! The 'seed' did not take long to grow. It was 'sowed' in at one end of the post office and 'reaped' at the other end the same day. The yield was about six hundred fold, enough for the balance on the house! With joy and praise to the Lord, we purchased the house, knowing it was the Lord's will for us to have it when He sent the needed balance. It became our home for the remainder of the years we spent in Blantyre.

Being settled in our house we were able to concentrate on the evangelism programme. An office was rented in the centre of Blantyre so that we could be easily contacted by church leaders and other interested members of the public. A young man, who had been recently converted, was appointed as office secretary on a full-time basis, receiving mail, sending out replies, providing information and materials for the NLFA activities.

As we knew that prayer was the most important basis for all other activities, we gave it the most prominent place in the yearly cycle. It was suggested that wherever two or more Christians lived near each other, or worked together, they should try to spend some time each day to pray for a number of people they knew who were not Christians. Then they were to look out for the Lord opening opportunities for them to witness to the ones for whom they were praying. Many of these small prayer meetings were held in villages, townships and homes.

Christians who worked in the offices, factories and shops in the towns and cities did not have a mid-day meal. People in Malawi usually had one meal each day, served in the evening and those working had a soft drink and a scone in the lunch period. As there was free time left the Christians felt that it would be good to organize lunch-hour prayer meetings.

One commenced in Blantyre with two people, but soon the numbers grew until they could not all meet in one place. They divided into groups, meeting in different offices and public places. It was estimated that eventually about 450 were meeting for prayer in the city during lunch periods! The idea spread to other business areas of the country, so prayer was the hub, around which the rest of the programme turned.

How New Life For All developed

The spokes of the programme then rotated around the hub of prayer in Malawi. The aim was not to transplant a programme which had been developed in Nigeria or in Latin America. We wanted it to be a seed which grew naturally in Malawian soil, its growth directed by local Christians who were led by the Holy Spirit.

First, there was a month set aside for the leaders in a congregation to pray and decide on the way the Lord wanted them to do outreach.

Second, another month was used to inform the local members of the congregation about the plans which had been suggested. It has to be remembered that parishes or congregational areas in Malawi are very large, sometimes up to 350 square miles, and the Christians in a congregation met in many different prayer-houses on Sundays, so information took some time to reach the scattered members.

Third, three months followed with Bible teaching and memorising of Scripture on a weekly basis, the purpose being that church members would find out from the Bible teaching, the importance of being born again themselves. They had to know the Lord Jesus personally through the Holy Spirit, and the power which He gives to witness or they would not be able to introduce others to Him. They had to understand from Scripture why Jesus told His disciples not to go out witnessing without the power of the Holy Spirit (Luke 24:49 and Acts 1:8). The memorising of Scripture was necessary so that the person could use the Word in witness.

Fourth, a period of five months of outreach when those who had gone through the twelve weeks of Bible study were given cards authorising them to be involved in house-to-house visitation, open-air witness teams, and the distribution of NLFA gospel literature. The government required that cards should be carried by NLFA participants in outreach, as the Jehovah Witnesses had recently been banned in Malawi and the government feared that they might use the cover of NLFA to propagate their doctrines.

In fact, some of the Christians were reluctant to get involved in outreach at first as they said only Jehovah Witnesses did that. It had to be explained to them that the early Christians went 'everywhere' talking about the Word and what it said about Jesus (Acts 8:4). Those were the ordinary Christians, not the church leaders as they were still in Jerusalem (Acts 8:1). The word for 'preaching' in that verse is a word which means 'talking'. Any Christian should be able to talk about Jesus!

Fifth, the month following the period of outreach was spent in follow-up of interested contacts and especially with those who found the Lord Jesus as their Saviour. The object was to make sure that they had been introduced to a spiritually alive fellowship of believers.

Sixth, the last month of the twelve was used by the minister or pastor and his congregational leaders to prayerfully evaluate the year's programme – finding out mistakes made, what had proved successful, and what seemed especially blessed by God. Then on the basis of these findings, they would consider what should be done the following year.

Seven, as the hub of the cycle was prayer, the prayer meetings continued throughout the whole year.

The cycle was designed for a year, but not necessarily a calendar one. In Malawi there are five or six months of rain, November to May, and the rest of the year is free from rain. It was best to plan the programme in such a way that the first five months would be during the rainy season as the activities were all indoors, and the outreach could then commence in the dry season and make it easier to put into practice the outdoor activities. A good time to start the yearly cycle was in November.

During the year, retreats were held in different parts of the country when the Christians were urged to meet together to share their experiences and to hear some exhortations on how to be more effective in their witness. The retreats gave opportunities to encourage and inspire the Christians in their conflicts with evil as they searched for the 'lost sheep' and the 'prodigals'. Many of them were young Christians who had only recently come to know the joys of salvation themselves.

I had the joy of sharing in many of these retreats with enthusiastic soul-winners. We would deal with a subject like 'Fishing for men', illustrating the points with 'parables' or stories, as Jesus often did when He preached or talked. For instance, the fact that if one wants to catch fish one must go to where there are fish was illustrated with the incident I have mentioned when I found Ruth 'fishing' in the bath water and when Peter fished all night and caught nothing. I pointed out that it is wrong to think that we can only fish for people in church. Most of those who come to church have already been caught. Some may be smoked fish, and some may be frozen fish, but they have been caught. It is our responsibility to 'launch out into the deep', as Jesus told Peter. There are many out there who never come to church.

We do not read that Jesus 'caught' as many people as His followers in the Book of Acts. He found the fishermen by the sea, the Samaritan woman by a well, Matthew in his office, Zacchaeus up a tree, the sick man by the pool, Bartimaeus on the road side, and Mary Magdalene at a party.

The second important point that was discussed on the subject of fishing for people was the fact that to catch fish the correct bait must be used. I used an experience I had to illustrate that truth. One day I fished for two hours in a Malawi dam and caught no fish. A small boy came up to me and asked, in the local language, 'Have you caught any fish?'

I said to him, 'I have not caught any fish.' I then asked, 'Are there any fish in the dam?'

'There are plenty of fish in the dam,' he replied.

'Then why am I not catching any?' I enquired.

The boy did not have much education, perhaps he had never been to school, but he knew a lot more about fishing than I did!

'What kind of bait are you using?' he asked.

When I showed him the type of insects I was using, he shook his head and said, 'The fish in this dam do not know that bait.'

I asked what kind of bait they liked, and he pulled a worm out of a tin he was carrying, and said, 'This is the kind of bait the fish like.'

He then asked for my hook, and when I gave it to him he threw my old bait away and put the worm on the hook. In five minutes I had a fish. I was not foolish enough to continue to fish with my old bait, but asked the boy where I could find some of the worms. He showed me a spot below the dam. I went to the place, got down on my knees and did some digging until I had a supply of the worms. (It is good to get down on our knees and search before the Lord, if the bait we are using to catch men is unsuccessful). I fished for another two hours and caught ten fish.

The illustration was an introduction to the words of Jesus: 'I, if I be lifted up from the earth, will draw all men unto me' (John 12:32), showing how important it is to have the power of the Holy Spirit to help to lift up Jesus in our witness, so that He can draw people. He is the true 'Bait' who will attract men and women to yield their lives to Him.

Jesus did not say, 'Follow me and fish for men!' He said, 'Follow me and *I will make* you fishers of men.' That is why He emphasized to the disciples the need of the power of the Holy Spirit in their lives.

The importance of presenting Jesus to sinners is illustrated by experience with children. If we find that a small child is playing with a dangerous item like a razor blade or a knife and refuses to part with it, not realising how dangerous it is, we know that it would be foolish to try to snatch it from the child, especially if the child is holding it tightly. One of the best methods is to offer the child something it likes better, such as a sweet.

That is true in the life of sinners. They like sin and do not want anyone to try to snatch it away from them. If challenged they usually try to hold sin tighter, like the disobedient child. It is the duty, then, of the Christian witness to have the power and guidance of the Holy Spirit to lift up Jesus, so that He will become more attractive than sin. Just as the adulterous woman at the well who found Jesus became an evangelist the same afternoon and went to extol Him to the people of her town. She introduced more people to Jesus that day than some Christians do all their lives!

That was the object of 'New Life For All' in evangelism – to get each Christian to lift up Jesus to their relatives, neighbours and workmates. Satan can keep people from coming to church to hear about Jesus, but he cannot keep sinners from meeting Christians in the home, street, marketplace, and at work. Christians have more opportunities to introduce non-Christians to Jesus than the preacher who stands in the pulpit because the majority of sinners do not come to church to hear him. The pastor's main work is to feed Christians with the Word of God and to see them become mature servants of God so that they can go out into the world and lift up Jesus to outsiders.

Paul tells us that God appoints leaders in the church for different types of service. Among these he says there are evangelists and pastor teachers, and he points out why God has chosen to have them: it is 'for the perfecting of the saints, for the work of ministry, for the edifying of the body of Christ' (Ephesians 4:11). God's people are to do the 'work of ministry'. That is

God's plan for the ministry of the church, pastors are to feed and guide them, evangelists are to lead and teach them in the ministry of outreach. Without that emphasis a congregation becomes stagnant.

Myra's sudden call back to Scotland
During this initial stage of launching NLFA, we appreciated very much the help of Myra Leslie. She carried most of the responsibility of correspondence for the programme and handled the literature and materials needed. But one day at the end of 1972, she received a message asking her to make a phone call to her home in Shetland.

When she phoned, she received the sad news that her father had died. The family wanted to pay her fare to return for the funeral, so Myra left us feeling the death of her father very much. It was her intention of returning to Malawi again. However, not very long after her father's funeral, her mother took seriously ill and the responsibility of caring for her fell on Myra's shoulders. She did not have the opportunity to return to Malawi.

After some time, she married a friend she had known from childhood, but they were only married for four years when Myra died very suddenly with a thrombosis.

Fruit from 'New Life for All'
After twenty five years the programme of NLFA is still functioning in Malawi and recent reports state that it is expanding to other congregations. There have been many outstanding conversions reported during the years as a result of individuals witnessing personally. I would like to refer to just two accounts of such.

A woman witchdoctor was contacted by a woman who witnessed to her about the Saviour's love and concern for her and the wonderful life she could live as one of His followers. The witchdoctor was wonderfully converted and threw away all her paraphernalia of the occult into the river. She then joined Christians in outreach to other non-churchgoers, and the last time I saw her she was standing outside an open-air market, telling people about the great change Jesus had made in her life. Being well known as a witchdoctor, her testimony was very effective.

One of Malawi's first graduates, Clement, the son of a Presbyterian minister, was sent overseas to study before Malawi had its own university. When he returned to the country with a Bachelor of Commerce degree and a diploma in statistics, he was appointed to a high post in the civil service. His colleagues tempted him to have a 'social drink' with them, otherwise he would not be socially accepted. At first he refused, saying that as the son of a minister, his father had never allowed intoxicating liqueur in the manse.

After some time Clement yielded to their pressure, but sad to say, in a short time he became an alcoholic and embezzled government money from the office to purchase liqueur. His fraud was discovered and he received a prison sentence of two years. When he came out of prison he had lost his job and he went deeper into alcoholism and lost all hope of recovery. In the meantime his wife and children were suffering from lack of food and clothes. At that stage one of the young men from the local church, Willie, who was a member of a 'New Life for All' team, decided to visit him. At first Clement was adamant that his case was hopeless. He said to Willie, 'It is useless for you to try to help me. You are wasting your time. I have tried and tried to break this habit but it is too strong for me!'

Willie continued to visit him, asking the Holy Spirit to draw Clement to the Saviour who could change him. Then during one visit the great transaction took place. Clement invited Jesus into his life and from that moment he never had any desire for alcohol again. He got involved in the church, began to attend NLFA evangelism training classes, and became very effective in winning others to Christ.

After two years, we were able to succeed in persuading the local manager of a firm of accountants to take Clement on to his staff as he had a Bachelor of Commerce degree. The manager only agreed to take him for a six month trial period when he heard that Clement had been an alcoholic. He gained rapid promotion. A local paper printed his story which caused widespread interest in his transformed life and brought many to him for spiritual help. The manager did not contact me at the end of the six months – Clement was a senior member of staff by that time. After twelve months, the manager sent a message asking, 'Have you any more young men like Clement?'

One day I found out the secret of Clement's wonderful success in winning men and women for Christ. He told me, 'Each morning when I pray, I say to the Lord, "Please send someone to me today who will ask me a question or in some other way give me a natural opening to witness for You." The Lord always answers my prayer!' Clement did not want to 'push religion down people's throats' and turn them away. He practised what the writer in Proverbs 11:30 emphasized, 'He that winneth souls is wise'.

We tried to urge all those involved in witness to follow that example and pray each day for opportunities to open up in which they could speak naturally about their Friend, the Lord Jesus, just as freely as they would talk about a member of their own family.

I have to report, sadly, that after a few years of fruitful service Clement died of a massive heart attack. We could only conclude that he was 'ripe for heaven' and that the Lord needed him for some duties there. But the influence he left behind is still bearing fruit. His last act on earth before he collapsed was to lead his children in memorising Scripture verses for Sunday School.

One other result of the NLFA programme should not be overlooked. Many of those who were involved became leaders, ministers or pastors in the church of Christ. From one of the lunch-hour prayer groups, four of the young men trained for the ministry.

'New Life for All' in Zambia

The churches in Zambia were interested in NLFA developments in Malawi and I was invited over to share some of the details with them. Willie Musopole, the church elder, who was instrumental in leading Clement to the Saviour also joined me on the trip. We felt it would be good for the church there to get a view from a layman's position as well as mine from the organizing secretary's angle.

The evangelical churches there decided to use the programme, feeling it would be a very effective way of reaching the thousands of copper miners and their families by the personal witness of the Christians with whom they lived and worked. Of course, Willie and I were only there to explain the programme and Malawi did not become involved in any way with NLFA's organization in Zambia.

18

Literature and Evangelism

With times of reviving in the church and many turning to the Lord for salvation, a problem grew very acute. How were these converts to be fed on 'the sincere milk of the Word' which Peter emphasizes is so important for young converts (1 Peter 2:2)? How were they to be instructed as well as fed, so that they could grow into mature Christians? Paul points out how important that must be in our ministry. He described its object: 'Till we all come in the unity of the faith, and of the knowledge of the Son of God, unto a perfect man, unto the measure of the stature of the fulness of Christ' (Ephesians 4:12). Converts must be led from the 'milk of the Word' to 'strong meat' which we are told in Hebrews 5:14 'belongeth to them that are of full age'.

What made the problem so acute was the fact that there were so few ministers and pastors to feed, instruct and guide young Christians from the Word. When we discussed the problems of evangelism in an earlier chapter, we noted that a full-time minister can average thirty prayer houses in his parish as it may be spread over an area as large as 350 square miles. Services in these prayer houses are taken each Sunday and midweek by elders, apart from the very few times the minister can visit a prayer house.

The need for literature in our ministry arose in the 1950s, and Isabel and I compiled the book of twelve Bible Studies entitled *Following Jesus*, written especially for converts. But in the 1970s a great need arose for help to be given to the elders who were struggling week-by-week to feed and instruct the section of God's church over which they had been made overseers. There was not much opportunity for secondary education in Malawi up to that time. Less than 10% of those who passed through primary school could find places in secondary schools, and as fees were required for both schools many large families could not afford the cost.

Therefore any type of theological education given to these men to help them in their ministry had to be simple for three reasons: they had to be able to understand it; they had to be able to use it; and it had to be easy to translate into the local language.

That great need was also felt in other African countries and the 'Evangelical Association of Africa and Madagascar' launched a programme of 'Theological Education by Extension' (TEE) to assist in the training of lay people in their own village situation. A committee was set up composed of representatives from evangelical missions and churches over a wide spectrum of the continent of Africa. Its members decided the courses should contain basic Bible doctrines, surveys of books of the Bible they felt would be most helpful, and practical teaching such as 'The shepherd and his flock'.

I was asked to help prepare the basic text for the course. The Association arranged for about twenty who had been asked to be writers of the text to travel to Harare in Zimbabwe where we were accommodated for a month. We had instructors who suggested that we only use an English vocabulary of not more than eight hundred simple words. We were taught the method of 'programmed instruction' where each short section or paragraph had to contain an important point of instruction, with a question on that point at the end of the section and a space for an answer. The next section started with an answer to the question, so that the student could check if he had understood. When studying a paragraph he was expected to put paper over the next section until he had tried to answer its question. If wrong, he had to go back over the previous section and study it again.

For the basic text, I was asked to enlarge *Following Jesus* into ten weekly sections, with five lessons for each week. The plan was that there would be a tutor appointed for each group who would meet with them each week and go over any problems encountered. The tutors were to be trained by the minister. The 'Theological Education by Extension' books are published by Evangel Press in Kenya.

The latest feedback from the publishers on *'Following Jesus for Theological Education by Extension'* states that the book has now been printed in over thirty languages. The text was designed to help lay preachers to feed and instruct their flock on the way of salvation and how to live the Christian life of service to Christ. However, reports have come back that it has resulted in a number of lay preachers themselves obtaining an assurance of their own salvation. Any member of the public is welcome to register for the courses – both men and women.

A further request came from 'Biblecor' which produces Bible Correspondence Courses organized by the Mission of the Dutch Reformed Church in South Africa. I was asked to produce a fourteen-lesson correspondence course on *How to be a Happy Christian*. Over 80,000 copies of the course have been printed in English and seven other languages used in Southern Africa. The examiners of the returned papers state that many studying the course have come to know the Lord Jesus Christ as their personal Saviour, for which we give the Lord the praise and glory!

Early in the 1980s the committee of the Nkhoma Synod Woman's Guild of the Presbyterian church in Malawi asked me to write a series of Bible Studies for their fortnightly meetings, to cover the whole year. The studies had to be in simple English for easy translation. The course was entitled *How to be a Fruitful Christian*, based on John 15.

When they were prepared, I was asked to record them for

205

broadcasting on Trans World Radio and later to have them published in English as the original copy in English was in photocopied form. It was only in 1994 that I was able to see that request materialize. The studies were published by Christian Focus Publications entitled *Effective Christian Living*. The simple English was retained, so that it could be used by those whose knowledge of English is limited, and also so they could be easily translated into vernacular to help lay preachers.

The publishers have also made it available in western countries and there are reports of it being used for personal devotion and by Bible Study groups in Britain. 35,000 have been printed in English so far, 25,000 specially for Kenya. There are requests for permission to translate it into Spanish, Zimbabwean languages, and Braille and large print for the partially blind.

The importance of Christian literature cannot be overstressed in both the work of evangelism and in the building up of converts into mature Christians. Sermons are needed, but sometimes they go in one ear and out the other, while the Word of God expounded on paper may lie for days or years, until in God's time, it is used by Him to impress a message on a soul. It also provides material for Christians and preachers in countries where they cannot hear the author in person, and where such books and magazines are very limited and expensive.

19

Ministry in the Capital City

In five years of involvement with 'New Life for All', we saw the programme established in Malawi, and I had attended conferences in Kenya and Zambia, as well as introducing it to ministers in Zimbabwe. We then concluded that the Lord was showing us the time had come to hand over the responsibility for its future to African colleagues. There was a danger that the churches might look on NLFA in Malawi as a European idea. We wanted it to be looked upon as natural to Africa in general, and to Malawi in particular.

The Evangelical Fellowship released me in September 1975. Willie Musopole, who went with me to Zambia, was secretary of the 'Evangelical Fellowship of Malawi' at that time and was appointed chairman of the NLFA committee. I can confirm that the programme is still very much alive in 1996, and producing spiritual fruit after twenty-six years!

When Dr. Hastings Banda came to power in Malawi, he decided that the capital of the country was in the wrong place. It was in the town of Zomba in the southern region, forty-two miles north of Blantyre, the commercial capital.

Blantyre became the first mission station of the Church of Scotland in the southern region in 1876, and was named after Blantyre in Scotland, the birthplace of David Livingstone. At that time there was no British Governor in the country. The area had only been discovered by Livingstone a few years earlier. Britain appointed a Governor in 1892 after the mission was well established. The Governor intended to have his headquarters adjacent to the mission, as Blantyre had become a centre of population in the sixteen years that the mission had been operating. People had moved there because of the medical and other services available. Also it had become a haven for escaped slaves, as Arab slave traders were still capturing people in the country at that time. Moir Brothers from Scotland had also set up a commercial business, The African Lakes Corporation, selling groceries and hardware.

The Governor did not succeed in establishing his headquarters there. He found that the missionaries had won the confidence of the people to such an extent that they were looked upon as those who governed the country, and he was ignored. He decided to move forty-two miles and made Zomba the Capital. It remained the capital for the British administration for over eighty years, until Dr. Banda decided to change its position after the country's independence.

You may be wondering what all this history of the old Nyasaland has to do with the title of this chapter – let me explain. The town chosen for the new Capital was Lilongwe, a town with a population of 9,000 in the central region. A large area of land was taken over, east of the town for the new Capital City, and building commenced in 1973.

The Church of Central Africa Presbyterian (CCAP) was a union of the churches established by the missions of the United Free Church of Scotland, the Church of Scotland and the Dutch Reformed Church of South Africa. The denomination looked ahead and decided that a large church should be built in the Capital City, as it would be needed for the expanding population. The Mission of the Dutch Reformed Church in South Africa raised the money to build a church seating 1,200.

The local Synod of the CCAP knew that the ministry in that church would have to be different from the services held in the local churches where only the ChiChewa language was used. The Diplomatic Corps, United Nations staff, government officials, business and other international organizations would be based in the City. It was decided that services would be held in ChiChewa and in English, and that there would be an associate ministry of African and missionary ministers.

It was because of the plan for that congregation that my new ministry commenced. I was called to be an associate with an African minister in the new charge called Lingadzi CCAP. There were three other CCAP congregations in the city. They had been established for many years in the old town, before it had been taken over as part of the new capital.

I was inducted in September 1975, just as different government ministries were beginning to move into their new offices in the growing city. It was a wonderfully exciting time as my co-minister and I launched into ministry in the new extension charge. In five years it grew to a congregation with a membership of 3,000. Different ministries moved into the City bringing staff, who in many cases were church members already. The other three congregations which had been incorporated into the City also grew rapidly, as the town which had a population of 9,000 in 1970 became a city of over 100,000 by 1979.

The ministry in the city was unusual. Most of our work in Africa up to that time was in the field of evangelism, apart from the time I spent church planting in South Africa. I had taken quite literally Paul's command to Timothy to 'do the work of an evangelist' (2 Timothy 4:5). God's call to the new congregation combined both evangelism and pastoral work. In fact, the denomination gave me one third of my time free to help other ministers and pastors with evangelism.

In the new congregation, the difficulty was not to get people into church. But many of those who came were nominal church members without a personal relationship with Jesus as their Saviour. That meant there was need for evangelism in the congregation, as well as pastoral teaching and care of those who had experienced the new birth.

We had people from eighteen countries attending the English services. An average service was made up of one third white and two thirds black worshippers who knew English. I found that the people in our congregation came from ten denominations, as our church was the only one in the city that had an English service apart from the High Anglicans and the Roman Catholics. The Baptist Mission had an evening service, but it was mostly attended by their staff. Because of the situation most of those in the city area who came from an evangelical background worshipped with us, as well as others who were interested. Our organist was a Baptist and the Sunday School superintendent a Plymouth Brother! The church's multiracial session was made up of elders from different countries.

One of the difficulties we experienced was that some of those who came from the different church backgrounds, preferred the order of service of their own denomination! With so many church backgrounds that could not be done. For instance, those from Ireland thought the saying of the creed was Roman Catholic, but others from South Africa felt the service was not complete without the reading of the creed and the commandments in each service! We knew how much an order of service meant to Christians so we varied the order from time to time, which was acceptable to the congregation.

When we first arrived, there were no manses for the ministers. We had to live in other mission houses in the old town which were quite far away from the church. As the months past, the other minister and I found that situation frustrating because many of the Africans had no means of transport and we were isolated from them. The Synod had promised to raise the money to build the manses eventually, but there was no evidence of any start being made. Things came to a head when the City Corporation notified us that the two plots, which they had reserved for manses, would not be held any longer unless steps were taken in the near future to commence the building work.

We suggested to the session that we should immediately

start a 'Manse Fund' and keep the account in the bank in our own congregation's name, so that headquarters would not use it for some other emergency need, as can happen in African church life! Session, and then Synod, agreed and the fund was launched. We found the project to raise the money for the manses was a blessing in disguise. When we announced the project to the congregation there was an immediate response. It was decided that a men's group and a women's group would be formed and meet to discuss ways in which they could help to see the Lord answer prayer for the money that was needed. We had to smile afterwards when the woman's group called themselves 'The Women's Action Group' and became known as WAG. Their tongues certainly did wag as they knitted and cooked for the fund.

As mentioned, the congregation was multiracial, but the white and black races had their own townships in the new City. Some of the more wealthy Africans and those who were top government officials were able to buy or rent the more expensive houses in areas which were mostly occupied by white people. But to a great extent the two races lived separate lives during the week. There was not much opportunity of getting to know each other by only attending the services, but the working groups for the 'Manse Fund' brought them together in a new way. White men with top international positions were involved with black men from humble walks of life. Wives of Ambassadors and High Commissioners as well as others in the diplomatic, commercial and international organizations were mixing with wives of humble labourers. Sometimes they met in the South African Ambassador's double storey residence where the African women were fascinated with stairs and other luxurious fittings which they had never seen before.

They had a monthly sale at one of the supermarkets of items they had knitted and cooked. The men made toys and other items for children. Isabel and I were not keen on church sales before this as we thought that Christians should give directly to the Lord. But we saw the wonderful effect as these men and women got to know each other, producing a unity in the church which would have been very difficult to generate in any other way with people of different backgrounds. We were also encouraged by the account of the Children of Israel helping to provide materials for the tabernacle and temple.

Isabel was involved in the woman's group and had to put her 'foot down' on some suggestions, like one from a diplomat's wife who wanted a mannequin parade! When Isabel told her that the church would not agree, she was quite surprised and told Isabel, 'We will never get the money we need for the manses, unless we do things like that.' When Isabel returned to the manse after that meeting she found a letter with a donation of £800 for the manses. She rang the lady right away to tell her how the Lord answers prayer in His own way, without doing questionable things.

There was another result from the work groups. When Synod saw the determination of the congregation to work for the manses, its committee got in touch with the Mission of the Dutch Reformed Church in South Africa which had raised the money to build the church. Two large donations were received from there, as all the missionaries working in that Synod area came from South Africa, apart from two lady teachers and myself who were Irish and a lady teacher from Scotland.

The Presbyterian Church in Ireland donated a large sum to the manse fund and in a number of months we had the equivalent of £40,000, the sum which the mission builder estimated would be needed for both manses. Building work commenced and in about six months we ministers were able to move into our new manses. The day Isabel and I flitted the wife of the South African Ambassador arrived with a large container. She said, 'I have brought your lunch. I am sorry that we could not invite you to the residence for a meal today as we have an official function, but before I leave I would like to help you to lay your carpets.' We had to inform her that we did not have any carpets! She then added: 'I will scrub the lounge floor for you,' which she proceeded to do, down on her knees. It was a concrete floor! Afterwards we found enough food in the container she had brought to last us for a few days.

We had many meals in their official residence after that. Some of these times were official functions where the Ambassador, who with his wife faithfully attended the services, would not only ask me to say grace, but then ask us both to tell the company at the table some of the highlights of our missionary work.

There was one other extension project in which the congregation and Synod co-operated. The tenants of a large ground-floor shop immediately behind the church and standing in its own grounds were moving out to new premises which they had built. The building was owned by the City Corporation. We felt that it would be ideal for our church hall which we thought would have to be built in the near future.

I approached the City Corporation Property Department regarding their plans for the building and was informed that they intended letting it to a child welfare organization. They suggested that if we would buy the building, we could arrange with the welfare people to use it as they only wanted to use it in daylight hours on weekdays and the rent they paid could help our church funds.

The price they suggested was the equivalent of £20,000 in Malawian currency, but after a little talk they reduced it to £15,000! It was a stretch of our faith to decide to buy, but the Lord provided and the building became the church hall and is still being used for Sunday School, and other church meetings.

There were many expatriates in the city who did not come to church and I felt it was my responsibility with my background in evangelism to do all I could to find the 'lost sheep'. One of the methods used was to ask those who were coming to church to inform us if there was any one they knew who was not coming, but who might appreciate a visit. That led to interesting contacts.

One lady gave me the address of an Ulster couple. She said the wife would be interested, but she was not sure that the husband would be. I went to their home one Saturday afternoon and found the husband Jim sitting on the veranda listening to a football match on the radio. After greeting him, I said, 'I have come round to hear an Irish accent.'

'From where have you dropped?' he asked.

'I am one of the ministers in the new church, and friends of yours thought that it would be good for me to call and see you and your wife, as we come from the same country.'

He called his wife Jean and we had a chat over a cup of tea. Then Jim said, 'You will see us both in church tomorrow!'

True to his word, they were in church the next morning, and from that time they never missed a service when able to attend.

Not only did they attend, but as Jim was the clerk of works for a very large government building scheme, he became a great asset in the church with his practical help. He made a lovely board for the front of the church, showing times of services etc., and he also helped with jobs that needed to be done in the new manses and hall. Isabel and I are still in touch with the couple who now live near Belfast.

One evening, just as we were about to leave the manse for the official opening of an ambassador's residence, our front door bell rang. We found a young Japanese man on the door step, holding a copy of the Good News Bible. He bowed low in the usual Japanese mode of greeting and said, 'I have come to ask if you would please explain this book to me?'

I told him that we were just about to leave for a function, but if he gave me his address I would be glad to visit him.

We arranged an evening and I spent four and a half hours with him. His name was Toshi. I found that he had been brought up in the Buddhist faith. He was a civil engineer, and had been sent by the Japanese government with others to assist Malawi in its development. He was working with the water department and was surveying a catchment area for a new dam near one of our mission stations. One of the Irish missionaries on the station had given him the Bible and he had gone to his superior in the water department, who was a British engineer, asking him to explain the 'Book'. Unfortunately the engineer was more interested in the 'bottle' than the Bible, and he suggested that Toshi should go to the manse! That was how he contacted us.

What a wonderful joy it was for me to go over God's way of salvation with him, and to see him sitting there gazing at the verses which showed how Jesus had come to earth and suffered such a cruel death so that we could be forgiven and changed into new persons. Finally he said, 'I always thought that Jesus died because he was a criminal. I did not know that He was the Son of God who had no sin and that He died for us!'

I went on to point out that Jesus knocks at the door of our inner self, and that when we invite Him, He comes in forgiving and transforming us. It was difficult to know how much of God's way of salvation he had grasped, and it is never my policy to urge a mere head belief in Christ without an intelligent full commitment of one's will and life to Him. I urged Toshi to pray to God after I had left and ask Him to make clear the meaning of the verses we had read and to show him how to accept Jesus as his Saviour.

Toshi came back a few days later to tell me that he had put his faith in the Lord Jesus as his Saviour. From that time he attended the worship services and Bible studies faithfully. He was a good singer, but not knowing English very well, he would lean over Isabel's shoulder and echo the words!

As the Bible was a new book to him, at first it was very hard for him to find Scripture references, so he decided to make his own thumb index! He stuck little pieces of paper with the name at the beginning of each book in the Bible. I wish I could let you see his Bible after a few months. It showed that he had used it extensively. It was a wonderful day of rejoicing in the church when he came forward for baptism and was received into the congregation on profession of faith.

One day after he returned to Japan, he phoned to ask if I would fly to Japan at his expense to conduct the wedding ceremony for him and his bride, as he wanted it to be a Christian wedding! Unfortunately my programme did not allow me to go, but he had a Christian wedding and sent us a photo. More than a year later, I had a letter from the minister of a Presbyterian church in Japan in which he asked, 'Would you please send me Toshi Yoshida's baptismal certificate. He attends my church and wants to have his child baptised.'

Toshi and I kept up a correspondence for some years, and he came back once to see us in Malawi. But recently we have lost contact and I am not sure of the reason. Perhaps it is because we have moved around a lot since we left Lilongwe, and he does not know where to send me his new address, because he too has moved. I still pray for him and for renewed contact.

There were others we had the joy of welcoming into the Lord's house through different circumstances.

The wife of an official of the United Nations rang me in a very agitated state. 'My husband has ordered me out of the house, can you please come now?'

When I arrived in the house the atmosphere was tense. The fact that his wife had called me added to his anger! I eventually found out the reason for the disagreement. His wife had gone to an island in the Seychelles off the east coast of Africa to do scuba diving, while the husband went on holiday elsewhere.

A local person from Lilongwe happened to be on the island at the same time as the wife, and when he returned he told her husband he had seen his wife sitting on the beach with another man. She tried to explain to her husband that she had met the man in the hotel and he told her that he knew a very good spot to dive. He went with her to show her the place. The husband would not accept her story.

I sat between them on a couch for about four hours, doing my best to keep the husband from physically attacking his wife. When he calmed down a little, I tried to reason with him, pointing out he had no proof that his wife had done wrong, and how foolish it was to build up such a storm using his imagination.

Eventually he agreed to withdraw his accusation and asked his wife to forgive him which she did. I then discussed the way of salvation with them and they both prayed and asked the Lord to forgive them. They began to attend church, but it was only a short time afterwards when the husband had a heart attack and died on the golf course in Lilongwe. I led his funeral service, when many of the diplomatic corps attended.

I was so glad that their marital problem had been solved, as the husband was not only ordering her out of the house, but said he was changing his will so that she would not benefit from his estate. Had that happened, his wife who came from Germany would have been left destitute. He was a Canadian.

As the English service was held at 9.00 am on Sunday, we invited any of the congregation who wished to do so to come for refreshments and fellowship to the manse after the service. It was interesting to see how diplomats from Zambia and Nigeria as well as a doctor from Ghana would be sitting talking to the Ambassador from South Africa. There were sanctions against South Africa at the time, and these countries could not have official diplomatic relations with South Africa. The church was doing what the UNO found difficult to do!

We had the late Dr. John Gray and Mrs. Sheila Gray on an official visit to the city when he was Moderator of the Church of Scotland. He preached for us in an Easter Sunday evening service. We also had the privilege of having a reception at the manse for him and Mrs. Gray when people from many different countries were able to meet them. We were able to take them out to Nkhoma mission station, where they were very interested in the hospital and other mission work that was being done.

The congregation had the privilege of being asked by the British High Commissioner to organize a service in 1988 for the 25th anniversary of the Queen's coronation. It was attended by the Diplomatic Corps representing their different countries.

Having been in Lilongwe for over four years, Ruth finished secondary school in South Africa and wanted to do nurse's training in South Africa as most of her school friends were there. Her course would take at least four years and we were concerned that she had so little home life up to that time. When I received requests from two different congregations in Cape Town to consider a call to minister there, we concluded that the Lord was opening a door for us to have a home for Ruth in Cape Town during her late teens and early twenties – a place where she could bring her friends. She was accepted for training in Groote Schuur hospital, made famous by Dr. Christian Barnard, the heart transplant surgeon.

I accepted the call to a multiracial church in a suburb of Cape Town and we left Lilongwe on 3rd January 1980.

Our house in Blantyre was let during the years we were in Lilongwe and the rent was divided among evangelical organizations like Scripture Union, Gideons, Hospital Christian Fellowship and New Life for All. When we were leaving Lilongwe in 1980 and realised that the Lord was not calling us back to Blantyre, we sold the house to the Africa Evangelical Fellowship as they wanted a house there for a missionary family.

We considered that the money from the sale of the house did not belong to us, although the lawyer said that legally it was ours, because it had been given to us personally. We felt the money had been given to us to further evangelism and it should go to that purpose. It was divided up among the above evangelical societies.

20

Ministry in Cape Town

The church in Cape Town was a united Congregational and Presbyterian church, although the union was just a regional one, which needs explaining. The Congregational church in Southern Africa had taken over the London Missionary Society's work in the whole of Southern Africa – Botswana, Zimbabwe, Mozambique and South Africa.

From 1904 meetings were held between the Presbyterians and Congregationalists on the subject of union. However, it was mostly only talking until the 1970s and 80s when it seemed that an agreement was being reached. With that in mind the Cape Town Presbytery of the Presbyterian Church and the Regional Council of the Congregational Church there came to a local arrangement – a kind of grassroots union. The union allowed the churches to call each other's ministers and to have a joint membership. Any new churches built were called United churches, coming under the joint control of the Presbytery and Regional Council.

I was called to one of the locally united churches, which was a Congregational church. It was expected that the two denominations would unite officially in 1984 after eighty years of negotiations. Assemblies of both were held in the same city at the same time that year, expecting final approval to be passed by both and then they would move into a joint Assembly. At their Assembly the Presbyterians unexpectedly passed a resolution to oppose the union, and it has not taken place up to the present time.

The Presbyterian Church membership was white by a large

majority – twenty to one, I think – while the membership of the Congregational Church was fifty per cent black, forty five per cent 'coloured', and five per cent white. It was thought that the final decision of the Presbyterians to withdraw was caused by a twofold fear. The vote in a joint Assembly would be predominately black, and stipends and pensions were higher in their denomination. There could also have been a fear that they might have to tow the others financially! I was out of the country at the time and did not attend Assembly.

In the church where I was a minister, the majority of the members where white, but the membership was open to any race. The difficulty we faced was the apartheid system which forced different races to live in segregated areas, and the church was in a 'white' area. There was a section of the city, about five miles from the church, in which 'coloured' people lived. Those classed as 'coloured' were people of mixed race. The nearest 'African' township was nearly ten miles away.

These divisions made it very difficult for those of other races to get to our church, as transport was a problem, especially from the African township. There were two other obstacles. The church being in a white area caused it to be classed as a church for white people. Language was the other difficulty, the coloured people used the Afrikaans language in their services and the Africans their own vernacular. Our services used English as a medium.

One young coloured student who joined our church was persecuted in the Teacher Training College he attended because the other students considered that he had joined a 'white' church. He tried to explain that it was multiracial, but because it had a majority of white people, they gave him the choice of withdrawing his membership from the church or ceasing to hold office in the Students' Representative Council. He chose the church and his loyalty to Christ and was expelled from the Council.

We had some coloured members, but no Africans. However, our church took a special interest in a congregation in the African township, providing help for some of the poorer members of that church. We also arranged from time to time to bring the African minister and his choir over to take our evening service. Members of our congregation went in their cars to collect those who wanted to come. We had some very interesting sermons from the minister and wonderful singing from the choir, as Africans are famous for their harmony.

After the service we all met in the hall for refreshments and fellowship. Our ladies did some special baking for the group who always enjoyed eating with and talking to the white and coloured members of our church, as they very seldom had opportunities to mix with other races. Our church was also able to arrange for the African minister to get a church car.

There was no prayer meeting in the church, apart from times for prayer at other meetings. After some months I felt the time had come for us to arrange a special meeting for prayer. Unfortunately, it seemed there was some activity almost every night, either in the church or neighbourhood which made it difficult to find a free evening. But a time was found when there was nothing special being held – that was at 6.00 am on Thursday morning! We started the early morning prayer meeting and a number attended. There was an interesting development, a man who lived near the church, but who was not a member of our church, was quite fascinated when he saw people coming so early to pray. He decided he would attend as well, and he took responsibility to have the room ready in the mornings before we arrived.

A coloured lady came to me one evening under deep conviction She had not been attending our church, but she attended a meeting at which I was speaking in the city. She told me the sad story of an event that took place one day when an anti-apartheid group was demonstrating. She saw a white policeman shoot dead a little coloured girl who was in the crowd. As a result, bitterness and hatred had been springing up in her heart against all white people, and she wanted the Lord to forgive her and cleanse her from such a spirit of hatred and anger. We had prayer together and she received the assurance that the Lord had answered her prayer and forgiven her. She with her husband and their children began to attend our church and later they became members. Her husband is now a minister and other members of the family are in Christian service.

One Sunday evening, I noticed a lady in the service I had not seen before and, although I shook hands with her at the door, she rushed away before I had a chance to talk to her. Later I asked one of the young ladies if she knew the visitor. She said, 'No, I followed to speak to her, but she walked too fast for me.'

The next evening the lady came to the manse, asking if she could have a talk. She told a heartbreaking story. Her husband, to whom she had been married for many years, had been seduced by a woman who was his boss in the business in which they worked. The marriage was breaking up, and she was completely shattered; she seemed on the verge of a nervous breakdown.

She said, 'I noticed your church one day and was drawn to attend a service. Now I know why. I am able to share the load I am carrying with someone who can pray for me.'

I was able to point her to the One who had died for her on Calvary and was now willing to come into her life as her Saviour if she invited Him. He would go with her on the journey of life as her Friend and Comforter, regardless of what happened. With tears she accepted Jesus as her Saviour and promised to follow and serve Him.

I worked quite hard at the time to see if the marriage could be saved by trying to see her husband and talking to him on the phone. But as I have found in so many other cases like that, it seems the seduced person is possessed by a spirit which no human reasoning can overcome. He needed the Lord, but did not turn to Him. I still pray for him.

Isabel and I had many meals and Bible studies with groups in her home after that. Although the marriage has not been healed, she has continued all through the years to serve the Lord in the fellowship of the church. She has been a deacon and has taken a special prayerful interest in visiting elderly people and bringing many of them to the services.

While I was in the church in Cape Town, the executive of the Congregational Assembly asked me to be convener of evangelism, knowing that I was interested in the subject. I had the opportunity of sharing talks on evangelism in different parts of the country, including a conference specially arranged for ministers at Rhodes University.

The four years we were there were difficult years for the churches in South Africa. The political situation in the country was becoming more and more critical and many church leaders were getting deeply involved in anti-government activities. As the white members of the Congregational denomination were only five per cent, a large majority of the members of the denomination felt that they should agree to civil disobedience and other ways of opposing the white government.

Our church became involved in the issue, although not because of a problem between the two races in the church. Rather our members were concerned about the political pressure which they felt was pushing out the spiritual life of the denomination. There were members in our deacons' court who thought that our church should withdraw from the denomination and become independent which some other churches had done. Others felt that it was our duty to remain and do all we could to maintain a spiritual influence in the denomination by prayer and seeking to see change in the country without violence. We were able to avoid the pressure to become an independent church.

In 1984 Ruth passed her general nursing and midwifery exams. We were very glad that we had been able to provide a home for her in the manse during that time. It was good to have her friends come to the manse and there are many of these friends with whom she still corresponds. At the time of writing, she is nursing in Scotland.

When her training was finished and there was no guarantee that she would remain in Cape Town as she could take an appointment anywhere in the country, we felt our reason for leaving Malawi no longer applied. I still had two years left before reaching the retirement age of the mission in Malawi. I enquired about the possibility of going back and was accepted for an appointment to teach at a lay-training centre for elders. After my farewell from the congregation, we prepared to leave the many warm friends who had supported us in our ministry. It was hard, though, to leave Ruth behind. Also my brother James and his family were engaged in mission work a few miles from the manse where we lived.

21

Return to Malawi

I travelled back by road to Malawi through Zambia and Mozambique We decided, however, that Isabel should fly as the situation in Mozambique was very unsettled at that time because of the civil war. It was just as well she was not with me because, both going into the country and leaving at the other end, I was ordered by soldiers to unpack everything in the car. While I was doing the unpacking one of the soldiers stood pointing a rifle at me! They were supposed to be checking if I had any weapons!

I could not obtain a travel visa at the border and was told that I would have to apply at Tete, the town on the banks of the Zambesi river which I had to cross in the centre of the country. I wondered what would happen if I was refused a visa when I had already covered half of my journey through the country by that time!

On my way to Tete I was stopped by a soldier. I wondered if he was going to demand that I unpack again, but when he came over to the car window he made signs that he wanted cigarettes, as he could not speak English. I also by signs explained that I did not have any, but I offered him some sweets which he was glad to receive. He then waved me to proceed. I breathed a sigh of relief and thanked the Lord.

At Tete I was interviewed by a Portuguese immigration officer who did not speak English, so it was a matter of using 'signs and wonders' again. He gave me a form to fill but when I handed it back to him he was very upset, pointing to the form and then my passport. Eventually I discovered that he was questioning the word Reverend in front of my name on the passport and why I had not included it on the form. He seemed to think I was passing off for another person, not filling in my full name! What a job I had explaining that it was not part of my name, but a title. By putting an imaginary 'dog' collar round my throat, it dawned on him that I must be a 'priest' as most of the Portuguese officers were Roman Catholics.

He then said, 'Come with me', as he proceeded to enter another room. I don't know if my heart missed a beat, but I felt weak. I wondered, am I about to be detained; has he mixed me up with some unwanted person? Some priests and ministers were very active in the politics of the civil war and were not welcome in the country! Also my passport was quite full of visas and immigration stamps and I wondered if I had been somewhere which made me a suspect. When we were settled in the room, he looked at me as I waited anxiously to hear what he was going to 'try' to say in his broken English.

'You missionaries not much money. Me no charge you visa,' and with a smile he stamped my passport. What an anticlimax! I realised then that he took me into the room so that other members of staff would not hear him. I went off with my passport stamped to meet the soldiers at the exit post on the border with Malawi, over a hundred miles away. I had the same treatment at gunpoint as when I entered; I wondered what they thought I would be taking out of Mozambique. My treatment by the Malawi customs was quite different. Just a declaration of what I was carrying, and as it was all personal belongings, there was no difficulty in getting through.

I was glad to reach the training-centre called Chongoni, having been four days on the way. I received a great welcome from the staff as I had known them when I was a minister in Lilongwe which was about thirty miles north. Some of our church conferences and the Synod meetings at that time were held there, but my role had changed from guest to staff member.

The centre had once been a tobacco farm and the owner on leaving the country gave it very cheaply to the mission which had converted it for training purposes. As well as being a training centre for elders and other officers in the Synod, it was also a conference centre which could be booked by organizations like Scripture Union, the Student Christian Organization, Gideons, and New Life for All.

At first the old farm buildings had been used for sleeping, eating and teaching, but as the years went past new buildings were erected. When Isabel and I arrived there was a dining room and kitchen, a large hall used for meetings and also serving as a chapel for devotional and worship services. A number of classrooms were attached to the hall and there were two separate dormitory blocks.

Two of the old farm dwelling houses were still used and Isabel and I were allocated to one of them; the other was occupied by an African minister. Our house was built of stone with very thick walls, with eight large rooms and a small dark kitchen. Isabel came close to having a very bad accident one day. She had just walked through a long corridor which connected the rooms and closed a door behind her when there was loud crash in the corridor. She wanted to find out what had happened but could not open the door again, the ceiling in the corridor had fallen down. The wooden supports which anchored it were eaten through by termite ants, so the beams, ceiling boards and heaps of clay from the ant tunnels fell. We were thankful that Isabel had not been a few seconds later.

We enjoyed our time at the training-centre, it was like getting back to the earlier days of missionary work again after being involved in pastoral work for almost ten years. The villagers from the areas around came with medical problems to Isabel, I extracted many teeth and we provided spectacles again.

Of course these activities had to be fitted around the training schedule. It was good to be in among the elders again. They worked in lonely villages with very little fellowship, isolated from opportunities to worship where their own souls could be fed and taught. How they enjoyed being together and under Bible teaching, as well as having the opportunity to ask questions and receive counsel.

I must admit, though, that the position was rather lonely for Isabel. There was no other lady missionary within ten miles. But once again she fitted into the work knowing that we were in the place the Lord had planned for us at that time. I admired her willingness under the circumstances.

It was not easy for many of the elders to come to the courses. Most of them had large extended families – their own children and grandchildren. There was quite a lot to do to prepare their gardens and to produce the food that was necessary for all the mouths that had to be fed. Also money had to be found to provide school fees, clothes etc. Others could not get the members in their prayer house to raise the money to pay their fare to and fees at the training centre. The more educated elders were teachers and civil servants and could only attend courses during holiday times.

Later the Synod decided that it was a better plan for those of us who were lecturing to go out to a centre in each Presbytery which made it easier for elders to attend. There were also two African ministers on the teaching staff.

It was interesting, from time to time, to welcome conference delegates and to see the enthusiasm of the young Christians of Scripture Union and the Student Christian Organization as they met for their annual meetings. It was also encouraging to know that they were eventually going out into positions in the nation as Christian men and women to witness for Christ.

The Woman's Guild, with their white blouses and black skirts created quite a show, as hundreds of them came for their annual conference. They seemed even more keen on Bible study than the men and that was saying a lot. They met during the year in their local prayer-houses fortnightly and always had a Bible study. It was at their request that I prepared the Bible Studies in the book *Effective Christian Living*.

The meeting of the Synod was a big event which took place every second year. All the ministers with one of their elders attended. The Synod was the ruling body of the church as the denomination had no Assembly. There is a General Synod, which does not have much say in the running of the five regional Synods apart from ministerial training and dealing with ministers who are under discipline.

I shall never forget the closing service of a Synod when a young minister gave the address. He had been away for a special course on how to counsel Moslems and lead them to Jesus and had been appointed to minister in a parish that was predominantly Moslem.

His subject in the service was the need to work today, because we 'know not what a day may bring forth' (Proverbs 27:1). That afternoon he left to travel to his parish, and to save his bus fare, he accepted a lift on top of a load of bags of maize on a lorry. His parish was on the lake shore and the road down to the lake had steep hills and sharp bends. The driver lost control at one of the bends and the lorry went off the road. The young minister died instantly in the accident.

What an emphasis his death added to his sermon. He did not know, and those of us who listened to him did not know, that that day was his last to work for his Master in this world – he did not know that heaven was awaiting him in the afternoon. That is one sermon that most of us who heard it will never forget. I believe that all of us who attended went back to our duties with renewed determination to work 'today', not knowing what another 'day will being forth'.

After we had spent a year at the Lay-training centre I was called to a congregation in Lilongwe. It was not the congregation in which we had ministered from 1975 to 1980, but one which had been established for many years in the old town of Lilongwe before the new Capital was built.

I was inducted in September 1985, but we knew that we would only be there for one year as I would reach the Mission retirement age in August 1986.

Lilongwe again

The congregation in which I was inducted in 1985 was known as the 'Old Lilongwe Congregation'. Unlike the Lingadzi one, where we had ministered in the 70s, it was not multiracial. There was no reason why white people could not join the church, but it was in an area predominantly occupied by Africans and a few Asians. As Lingadzi church was only three miles away, white people who attended church went there, although from time to time we had some who visited our English services.

The Church had the advantage of being close to four centres of education. There was a large girls' secondary boarding school, a university nurses' teaching college, a medical science school, and a police training school, as well as a hostel for young men who worked in the city.

There were three services on Sunday: an English service at 8.00 am, two in ChiChewa, the local language, at 10.00 am and 4.00 pm, and there was a also a ChiChewa service on Wednesdays at 4.00 pm. There was an African co-minister, who with the elders, was responsible for the ChiChewa services.

The English service was my responsibility and usually there would be at least five to six hundred at that service. Many in the congregation were students, but others were teachers, civil servants and office or shop workers who knew English. It was compulsory for the secondary school girls under school rules to attend a church of their choice, and as the majority came from families who were Presbyterian, we had a large group from the school in the services. Often a number of the girls would have practised a special hymn to sing for us.

Many of the trainee nurses from their college, who were not on hospital duties attended, as well as staff from the nearby hospital, and also young men from the Medical Science school which trained Medical Orderlies, Clinical Officers and Pharmacists. Malawi University did not have a full medical school at that time, and Clinical Officers, as already pointed out, were men who did not have entrance qualifications for overseas universities, but were trained to the position where they were able to do most of the work usually done by a fully qualified doctor.

By the time the English service was over, very often there were queues waiting at the doors of the church to enter for the ChiChewa service. Sometimes as many as twelve or fifteen hundred would crowd into the church for the 10.00 am service. Those who only knew a little English found that the 'Word tasted better in ChiChewa', as an old man in Scotland once explained to me why he liked to read the Bible in Gaelic. He said, 'It tastes better in Gaelic.' The church could not hold the whole congregation as the membership was around 3,000, so on Sunday mornings people met in a number of different places in the parish – in school rooms or halls.

During the time we were there we saw some Bible Study groups started in homes where a few Christians met together with the Word and to encourage one another. One of these homes stands out in my memory. I was called there by the wife who was very concerned about reports that were reaching her regarding her husband's interest in another woman. It was a well-to-do family with a lovely house, as the husband and some of the grown-up members of the family had very good jobs. Unfortunately the husband's government work took him away from home quite a lot and that was where he fell into temptation. His actions were bringing upheaval into what had been a happy home.

The husband, wife and I joined in a heart-to-heart talk and

prayer. They were both members of the church so we had the Word of God, and concern for His glory as a basis to examine the husband's unfaithfulness.

He admitted his sin and the fact that he knew it was wrong, and asked his wife to forgive him, promising her that he was ending the affair. At first she was reluctant to forgive, wondering if his expression of sorrow was genuine. But after he prayed and asked the Lord to forgive him, she was also willing to forgive. He professed faith in Christ and the marriage was healed. I had a Bible Study in that home each week for sometime afterwards. Almost ten years later, in 1994, when I was back in Malawi preaching at a 'Keswick' convention, the husband came to me and announced that he was still walking with Jesus and that he and his wife were still together, which was very encouraging.

We had an interesting weekend during our spell in the church. The Hospital Christian Fellowship was holding a special conference at the Nurses' College. Mr. Francis Grim, the main speaker at the conference, was asked to take our morning English service. As a result of the gospel message he gave, the Holy Spirit worked in a special way, and a number of those in the congregation went to him for counselling. Some professed faith in Christ and became involved in the life of the church.

I had a nasty experience while living in the manse there. Dr. Banda had an official residence close to the manse, with a stadium built into the grounds. Very often celebrations were held there when he was in residence. One Saturday there was a celebration in the stadium and crowds were passing the manse. I decided to take a photo so that people in Britain could see the crowds that were 'forced' to attend such gatherings. Anyone who did not attend was suspected of being subversive and could be detained immediately.

I stood in my garden and snapped a few shots. Suddenly a man walked out of the crowd into our garden and demanded that I go with him immediately to the police station! I told him that my wife was not at home and I would have to close up the manse. He said, 'Go and do that, but leave your camera outside the house.' I suppose he thought I might remove the film, if I took the camera into the house.

I was kept at the station for many hours. The police knew me, and although for security reasons a photo of the President was not allowed to be taken without permission, I had not broken the law as the President was not included in any of the shots I had taken. But the young man who had brought me to the station was one of the Malawi Young Pioneers, a paramilitary organization founded by Dr. Banda to protect his interests. They were armed and in the event of any uprising from the army they were to defend the President.

I think the police were afraid that if they did not take the Young Pioneer's action seriously, they might be reported, but they seemed to enjoy keeping the Young Pioneer sitting for a time to make him think twice before doing such a ridiculous thing again. The film was taken from my camera and I was allowed to go home. When the film was developed and printed, most of the prints were returned to me. A few were held back to save face, I think.

Isabel had a fright when she came home and read my note, stating that I had been taken to the police station because of photography, but she was greatly relieved when I came back!

There was another unforgettable incident that happened when we were in that manse. It was Christmas Day, 1985 and Isabel and I had just finished our Christmas dinner. We were discussing the fact that it was the first Christmas we had been alone for Christmas dinner for a number of years, when the telephone rang.

One of the missionary teachers phoned from sixty miles away at Lake Malawi with information that one of our missionary nursing sisters had been attacked by a hippo in the lake and was bleeding profusely. He asked me to go out to the mission station, about thirty miles away, and inform the doctors of the nurse's condition, asking them to come into the local hospital in Lilongwe. The telephone was out of order so he could not contact them. I will not disclose my miles per hour on the way to the station!

A number of missionaries were spending a few days together at the lake during the Christmas holidays, and the young man told me that they had been able to get the nurse out of the water and were arranging to bring her the sixty miles to the hospital.

When she arrived and Isabel and I saw her condition, we agreed that it would be a miracle if she lived. Just then Dr. John Phillips, who had been a Church of Scotland missionary, but was working in the government hospital at that time, arrived. When he realized that blood would be needed, he arranged immediately to draw some of his own for the patient.

The two mission doctors, with the surgical staff in the hospital, operated for five hours. Another mission sister and Isabel were asked to do the post-operative nursing of the patient, as the surgeon in the hospital said he did not have staff to take the responsibility for such a serious case. He said that she should be transferred to a better equipped hospital outside the country as soon as possible. That became very evident a few days later when Isabel saw a column of ants climbing up the leg of the bed. As she followed their trail she found they were proceeding under the bandages into the wounds!

The Mission gave the patient the choice of being flown to her home country of Holland or to South Africa, and she chose the latter. I was asked to arrange for the flight, but had difficulty as all the planes were fully booked. However one airline cancelled five bookings, so that there would be space for the stretcher, a doctor and a nurse.

The sister spent ten months in hospital and had to have a nerve graft in her leg. After convalescence and when she felt strong enough, although she has to wear a permanent ankle-support, she applied to go back to the hospital in Malawi again. At the time of writing, over ten years later, she still has a full-time sister's appointment in the hospital!

Knowing that I was fast approaching the Mission retirement age, Isabel and I were praying about our future. The Mission asked if we would not agree to stay on for an extra two years, but we felt that if we did, it would be more difficult for us to get involved in some useful work in Britain when we returned. We did not want to sit and do nothing when we reached that stage.

We knew that when we did return, we would have to face the fact that we had no house, no furniture, and only a very small pension. During all the years we were living by faith and trusting the Lord to provide for us without an allowance, no National Insurance stamps were paid. On hindsight, we can see that we should have had faith for their payment! The lack of payment meant that we would not get any state pension. When I was called to minister in the Church of Central Africa Presbyterian and received an allowance, there was no pension fund. I was supported by the South African Mission of the Dutch Reformed Church and the Mission had no scheme for pensions for British people. There would be a small pension as a result of the four years we worked in Cape Town.

Isabel's relatives are in Scotland and mine in Ireland. Both our parents passed away during the years we were abroad. The question was, To which country should we retire? But the Lord had not forgotten about us, as He promised, 'I know the plans I have for you' (Jeremiah 29:11). His plans began to present themselves after I met Captain Stephen Anderson, who was the Church of Scotland Evangelist at that time and was out in Malawi to speak at a Youth Conference. He knew that our time in Malawi was coming to an end and on returning to Scotland he contacted a minister friend who was the interim moderator of a vacant congregation in Sutherland, suggesting that the vacancy committee might be interested in giving me a call.

I received a letter asking if I would be willing to consider a call to Eddrachillis Parish in Sutherland. I also received a similar request from a congregation in Argyll. The two requests caused a problem. Being 6,000 miles away and not knowing the congregations, I knew I would have to say no to one, and perhaps both if we did not have the Lord's assurance about a call to either charge. After prayer Isabel and I decided that I should fly over to Scotland for two weekends and see the congregations. I was asked by both vacancy committees to preach and both gave me a 'sole nominee' request to preach again.

After conversation by telephone with Isabel across the miles, we decided that I should say no to Argyll and be willing to preach as sole nominee for Eddrachillis, if they were willing to wait until we returned. Another preaching appointment could not be arranged before I flew back to Malawi as a congregation must have two weekly announcements of the date when a minister will preach as sole nominee for a vacancy.

Being a minister of the Church of Central Africa Presbyterian, I contacted the Church of Scotland offices in Edinburgh to find out the position of accepting a call to a congregation in Scotland. I was informed that there was no difficulty in becoming a Church of Scotland minister as both denominations were members of the Alliance of Reformed Churches. There was a regulation of the Church of Scotland, though, that if a minister is over sixty years of age, an eligibility certificate must be obtained and it could only be given under exceptional circumstances! The committee for the ministry felt that the circumstances at Eddrachillis were exceptional as there had been a vacancy for a long time, and a certificate could be issued.

The secretary then went on to make things easier for us when he heard that I could not preach again before I flew back to Malawi. As I had preached at the morning and evening services in the vacant church, he said that if the congregation was willing to vote as a result of those services, it would mean that I did not have to preach again as sole nominee.

As a result of the secretary's suggestion the congregation voted, after a two-week notice, and I received a unanimous call to the congregation. The call meant that we would have a house when we returned and it settled the question as to whether we should return to Ireland or Scotland.

I was given my discharge by the Lilongwe Presbytery at a special farewell service and we left Malawi in September, 1986. We flew through South Africa, so that we could spend some time with Ruth as she still had a flat in Cape Town and was nursing in the city. We also saw my brother James and his family.

22

Return To Scotland

We arrived in Scourie in October, 1986 and were welcomed by the congregation. The charge had been vacant for about eighteen months, and the people seemed very happy to have their own minister and his wife again. We discovered there that when the Highland people professed faith in Christ they usually had weighed up the cost of discipleship and knew the standard of holy living that Jesus would require of them. During my pastorate, the relatively small church bought an organ and built a church hall.

Our daughter Ruth was married in the Scourie church in 1987, but returned to South Africa for some time. She has a son, Jonathan, and is now nursing in Scotland.

We knew from the beginning of our ministry in Scourie that we would be there for a period of five years at the most as I would reach the age of seventy in 1991, which is now the compulsory retirement age for a Church of Scotland minister. We were very sorry when the time came to leave and the congregation tried to find out if there was any way round the rule, but they could not find any. My farewell from the congregation took place on 9th of October, 1991.

Retirement

We retired to Inverness. However, I think the correct spelling of our retiring should be re-tyre-ing!

Since 1991 I have had five 'locum pastorates' in the Western Isles – twice on North Uist and once on Berneray, Lewis, Tiree and Coll. In addition there are many invitations for pulpit supply in the vicinity of Inverness and apart from a few Sundays, most are filled in that way. Five months have been spent serving in vacant parishes in the Inverness Presbytery.

I have returned to Africa three times. The first time was an invitation in 1989 to go for the Centenary celebrations of Nkhoma Synod. Then Isabel and I made a three month trip to South Africa in 1992/93. We stayed in Cape Town, but I visited Malawi for a short time.

At the end of 1993 we received an invitation to go back to Malawi for a two year period, to train elders in the Livingstonia area. Isabel and I felt it was too big a task to take on at our age, although we would have loved to accept. Our hearts are still in Africa! I offered to go for three months, while Isabel remained in Scotland.

It was wonderful to be back among our Malawi friends again, and I spent a busy, but very happy three months there in 1994. There were many more invitations for elders' training sessions in different congregations than was physically possible. Request after request reached me to extend my stay.

Through gifts given to me by interested people in Britain, I was able to buy seventeen bicycles to help ministers to travel around their parishes, and other bicycles were purchased later. I have already explained how large the parishes are and the problems the ministers face to get around to the prayer-houses.

I was very encouraged with the continued growth of the church. Because of the increase of numbers, congregations were dividing and new ones starting. As an example, one church I visited had divided when the membership reached 3,000, and formed three others. Now one of them has 3,000 members! A minister told me he baptized more than twenty adults each month over a period. When we first went to that region of the country in 1952 there was only one Presbytery, on my visit in 1994 there were eleven!

During my last week I preached twice daily at the Malawi

Keswick Convention, which was introduced by a radio service. On Sunday, I was asked to take the morning service in Lingadzi Church where we ministered in the 1970s.

After the service the elders approached me about the possibility of my going back to the church for two years, as they had no missionary minister. I told them it was something we would love to do, but thought at our age it would be difficult to fill the post because of the condition of our health.

They said, 'We have a manse and are willing to give you a stipend, if you will change your mind.' It was very distressing to me to hear their pleading and to see their great desire for the Lord's work in the city to go forward, and yet feel that we were not able to help them. The hunger for God's Word is great, but as Jesus said, the labourers are few. Ministers and pastors are stretched to the limit with such large parishes.

We continue to keep a missionary fund and have the joy of helping in different ways needy families. We maintain a large correspondence with African ministers and elders, sending literature and other items to help them in their work. After all, many of them are our own spiritual children and grandchildren! One year when we were on our way home, one of the converts said to us, 'Tell your people at home that you have a new son in Malawi.' I said to him, 'We want to see some grandchildren when we return!'

Isabel thought retirement would be a time of relaxation. I suppose it is my fault that it is not, because I am known as one who does not know when to say 'No'.